JO HARDY

with Caro Handley

Tales from a
Young
Vet

Mad cows, crazy kittens and
all creatures big and small

Certain details in this book, including names,
places and dates, have been changed.

HarperElement
An imprint of HarperCollins*Publishers*
1 London Bridge Street
London SE1 9GF

www.harpercollins.co.uk

First published by HarperElement 2015

13 5 7 9 10 8 6 4 2

A catalogue record of this book is
available from the British Library

ISBN 978-0-00-814248-3

Printed and bound in Great Britain by
Clays Ltd, St Ives plc

CHAPTER ONE

Critical Care and the Night Shift

'Can you help her? Please? She means the world to me. I don't know what I'd do without Misty.'

Tears filled the eyes of the elderly woman on the other side of the consultation table as she looked down at the small white ball of fur in her arms.

I took a deep breath.

'Pop her on the table and let's have a quick look.'

Misty was a little terrier, and she was clearly feeling pretty ill. She lay on her side on the table in front of me, whimpering and panting frantically. Terriers can be real rascals, full of energy, always keeping their owners on their toes, but poor Misty was obviously in a bad way.

I was doing my best to sound confident, but inside I was quaking. It was my first twelve-hour shift in Emergency Critical Care – the equivalent of accident and emergency for pets – at the world-famous Queen Mother Hospital for Animals, and it was my job to assess each new case as it came in and to judge whether the animal could wait for attention or needed to be rushed straight to the Emergency Room – or ER – for treatment.

This was crunch time. As a fourth-year vet student I'd done all the theory, attended endless lectures, written papers and taken exams; in fact, just about everything except take charge of real live animals. Now, I, together with the other 250 students in my year at the Royal Veterinary College, was starting the final year of training – a whirlwind of back-to-back work placements known as rotations in which we'd be taking all that we'd learned in the classroom and putting it to the test in practices, farms, zoos and animal hospitals. We'd be covering everything from surgery to radiology to anaesthesia and tackling a whole range of life-saving procedures for the first time. Each of our three dozen or so placements would be assessed – we couldn't afford to fail a single one.

I'd started out feeling a mixture of excitement and terror, anticipation and blind panic. What if I blew it, made a wrong diagnosis, failed to spot something vital or just froze? Was I really cut out to be a vet, or had I been fooling myself? It was time to find out. So here I was, in Emergency Critical Care, just three weeks into rotations, in at the deep end, dealing with a non-stop queue of very sick animals with very worried owners and having to make the vital first-stage triage assessments on my own.

That morning I'd got my kit ready – the unwritten vet 'uniform' of chinos, flat pumps and checked shirt. Over that went the student's purple scrub top with my name stitched onto the top left side, plus a stethoscope round my neck, thermometer, scissors, notepad and pens (lots) shoved in my pockets. And a fob watch, because as vets we had to keep our arms below the elbow bare of clothing or jewellery.

Knowing that I'd be on the front line of emergency animal care had kept me awake for a good part of the night. So far we'd had a couple of easy weeks, learning how to take diagnostic images and spending time in dermatology. But now, along with the four other trainee vets in my rotation group, I would be facing a continuous stream of animals, all needing a split-second diagnosis. Animals can't tell you what they're feeling, so all a vet can do is look at the presenting symptoms, the animal's condition and its history and put everything together to try to work out what's going on.

I looked down at Misty, trying to remember my list of vital checks and questions. A three-year-old West Highland terrier, she was clearly in distress. Her temperature was high and her heart was racing. Her face looked swollen and her breathing was becoming ever more laboured.

Her owner, Mrs Stevens, was clearly worried and distressed. I could see that Misty meant the world to her. In a shaky voice she explained that she had taken Misty to the park a few hours earlier.

'It was such a nice day,' she said, her voice wobbling with emotion. 'The sun was out, so we went for a walk and stopped for a bit. I sat on a bench and Misty was chasing around in the flowerbed. Then she yelped. I think she might have been stung by a bee. But surely that wouldn't make her so ill, would it?'

She had just given me the clue I needed. I was pretty sure it had to be anaphylactic shock – an extreme allergic reaction – and there wasn't much time to waste. The swelling was now so intense that Misty's tongue and gums were turning blue from lack of oxygen.

'I think Misty may have had a bad reaction to that sting,' I told her. 'Sometimes it can be very extreme. I'll need to take her through to see a senior vet. Try not to worry. You have a sit down and I'll ask someone to bring you a cup of tea.'

'Please do your best,' she said, her eyes filling again. 'I can't lose her.'

I carried Misty through to the treatment room, where I explained to the clinician in charge what I thought was going on. He agreed, and the team swung into action to administer oxygen via a mask, IV fluids and steroids. The steroids would reduce the inflammation in her mouth and larynx so that she could breathe properly again. A nurse ran to get a fan to bring down her temperature, which was still rising. As the team rushed around Misty I checked her vital signs – heart rate, respiration rate and temperature – so that we had a base line against which we could check, to see whether she was improving or deteriorating.

'Come on, Misty,' I muttered, looking at her prone form. 'Stay with us.'

After a tense hour she gradually began to perk up and I felt weak-kneed with relief. Along with a supervising vet I went back to see Mrs Stevens in the waiting room to let her know that Misty was starting to improve. We would keep an eye on her overnight and if all went well she would be on her way home the following morning.

Mrs Stevens clasped my hand, relief etched on her face. 'Thank you, oh, thank you. I can't tell you how grateful I am.'

'We're here to help and I'm glad we could,' I said. 'We'll be checking on her right through the night, so try not to worry.'

Seeing Mrs Steven's reaction I was reminded how much this job is about people as well as pets. Every animal belongs to someone who loves and cares for it. A dog or a cat becomes a member of the family, and sometimes they are also a treasured companion to someone living alone.

Back in the ER I took a gulp from the cup of tea I'd been handed half an hour earlier, now stone cold, and slumped into a chair. It looked as if it was going to be a long night.

As I finished my tea and stood up my best friend Lucy shot past, holding a very limp-looking poodle. 'Nasty V and D,' she muttered. Numerous cases of vomiting and diarrhoea appeared in the hospital, so the staff all knew it as V and D.

'You OK?'

'Yes, you?'

'Fine. Catch you later.'

It was the longest conversation we'd managed all evening. Lucy was in my rotation group, so we would be doing all our core placements together. Clever, forthright and outgoing, Lucy was a fantastic friend and she was going to be a talented vet. We'd clicked from the moment we met, in the third year, and had been close friends ever since.

The phone rang and I leaped to grab it.

'It's reception. We've got a lady here with a very poorly cat.'

'I'm on my way.'

I took a deep breath, rubbed my tired eyes, straightened my scrub top and headed down the corridor to the cat waiting area. The Queen Mother Hospital, known as the QMH, has a bank of reception desks and beyond them there are separate dog and cat waiting areas – for obvious reasons.

The QMH is situated on the campus of the Royal Veterinary College in Hertfordshire. It's a world-class, state-of-the-art veterinary hospital with superb facilities. Twelve thousand animals go through the door each year to be treated by a team of highly experienced vets. The hospital's daytime working hours are 7am to 7pm, but it offers a twenty-four-hour service. At night only the emergency department operates, so every animal that needs out-of-hours urgent care arrives there first, and more than any other service in the hospital it relies on students to keep it going. That meant long hours on our part; our shifts were midday to midnight, or four in the afternoon to four in the morning.

We trainee vets did the initial assessments of the endless stream of animals arriving overnight, but we then reported to a senior clinician and a couple of interns, qualified vets completing an advanced version of rotations to further their careers.

While we were the only ones on the spot, staff from other departments were always on call should they be needed, and the sight of a dishevelled surgeon, hair awry, shirt half-buttoned, hurrying through the darkened corridors towards the operating theatre to attend to an emergency was pretty common.

I already knew just how brilliant the emergency vets could be; my family's lovely springer spaniel Tosca had undergone life-saving surgery at the QMH the previous year, after getting into a sack of dried food and gorging on a large quantity that swelled in her stomach. The first surgery at our local vet practice had gone wrong, causing her abdomen to become septic. While a very ill Tosca was rushed into theatre, a final-year vet student, who had been impressively thorough and calm, had consulted with me and my parents.

It had seemed impossible then that just a year later I would be the one doing the consultations. But here I was, doing my best to appear calm and competent. In the waiting room I looked around. 'Pepsi?' A friendly-looking couple and their young son leaped to their feet as I approached.

'Pepsi isn't well,' said the boy, who was about ten. 'She keeps going to sleep and she won't eat.'

His mum joined in. 'She's been losing weight and now she just seems to have no energy.'

'And she's only eighteen months,' finished the dad.

'Right, well, let's go through to the consulting room and take a look at her, shall we?'

I was already beginning to realise that with more than one owner present, all keen to tell me what was going on, I was likely to end up having to untangle the story.

Pepsi was a sorry sight. She was a pretty little tabby, and she flopped on the examining table with no interest in anything going on around her. I took a look at her gums. They were practically white, a sure sign that she was anaemic.

I asked the family to wait and carried her gently through to the chief clinician, Giacamo, in the ER. Exuberantly Italian, outgoing and laid-back, Giacomo is a brilliant vet. He examined Pepsi and asked me what I thought.

'Her pale gums indicate severe anaemia.'

'And what do you think might be causing that in such a young cat?'

I hazarded a guess. 'Well, it's either loss of blood, a destruction of blood, or a lack of production of blood. Since there's no obvious haemorrhage, I think a good starting point would be to rule in or out IMHA – immune mediated haemolytic anaemia.'

'OK, can you tell me about that?'

'It happens when the cat's body is destroying its own red blood cells. But we would need to run blood tests to check.'

'Good, right, take some blood, get it down to the lab, have a look under the microscope, and come back and tell me what you reckon, fast as possible.'

I leaped into action, filling a small vial with blood from Pepsi's jugular vein. Many cats would object to this and miaow loudly, but Pepsi was silent and unresponsive.

'Don't worry little thing,' I said, stroking her head. 'We'll get you better.'

With no lab assistants there at night I needed to do the blood test myself. I hurried down the hospital's hushed corridors to the lab, smeared a few drops of blood onto a slide and looked at it through a microscope. Some of the red blood cells looked almost transparent; they're known as ghost cells. The diagnosis was right; Pepsi's body was behaving as though her own blood cells were foreign bodies that had to be destroyed.

Giacomo was back at my side. 'So, how do we treat it?'

'We could downgrade her immune system, but that would make her vulnerable to other diseases.'

'Or?'

'Give her a transfusion?'

'Yes, we'll need to ask reception to ring around for a donor. And in the meantime we'll give her the synthetic substitute. It might take a while to find a donor, and she can't wait.'

Along with one of the interns I went to explain to Pepsi's owners that she would need to be with us for a while and that she would need a transfusion.

'Why has she got it?' the mother asked.

'We don't always know. It can be triggered by something like a vaccination or certain types of drugs, but sometimes it just happens and the cause is unknown.'

I promised we would call with an update first thing in

the morning. The little boy smiled and waved to me as they headed for the door.

Back in the ER Pepsi was being given Oxyglobin, a synthetic substance that could be given to cats and dogs needing transfusions as a temporary substitute for donor blood. Within a few hours she was sitting up and looking around and her eyes had turned bright gold, a side-effect of the Oxyglobin that made her look distinctly weird.

Cat blood types are commonly A or B, and occasionally AB. It's dangerous to give them the wrong type – it would kill them – so we needed to find a match to Pepsi's A-type blood. The QMH had a long list of willing donors, but finding one meant ringing to ask the owners to bring their pet in to have blood taken. The whole process could take half a day or so, and given that it was now late in the evening, possibly longer.

Pepsi was taken through to the Intensive Care Unit and placed gently into a cage lined with a soft blanket, where the nurses would keep a close eye on her until it was time for her transfusion.

While I was there I nipped over to check on Misty, the Westie with the severe bee-sting reaction. She was fast asleep, her breathing was normal and so was her temperature. She would almost certainly make a full recovery, and I knew just how much that would mean to Mrs Stevens.

The new patients rolled in non-stop that night, and I would discover over the following week that this was the norm. We students would deal with a patient and then run to take the next on the list. It was so busy that after the first few cases I forgot all about my nerves; I just had to get on with it.

Adrenaline-fuelled, I was buzzing, with no time to stop or to eat. Around midnight Stacy, one of the interns, stopped me in the corridor as I headed back to reception for my next case. 'Take a break after this next one and get some sugar into you or you're going to collapse,' she said in a tone that brooked no argument. The interns and clinicians were well aware of how easy it was to forget to eat and end up making yourself ill.

That night I saw a dog with heart failure, another with unexplained bleeding and a cat with seizures. After each assessment I would report back to Giacomo or one of the interns, and we would discuss what might be wrong and what should be done.

More than once I had to hazard a guess under the fierce gaze of an intern waiting to know what my diagnosis was. Thank goodness most of the time I got it right – and each time that happened it boosted my confidence a little more.

Around one in the morning, after I'd wolfed a bar of chocolate and downed most of a cup of tea, the phone shrilled again. Off I went, hurrying back towards the waiting area to collect a dog I'd been told was in a lot of pain.

I could hear his howls and whimpers from the other end of the corridor. I arrived to find a young yellow Labrador lying on the floor yelping. His owner, wrapped in a huge parka, looked exhausted. He introduced himself as Doug.

'Barney's nine months old, he's normally the life and soul, but he's not been himself today,' Doug said, raising his voice to make himself heard over Barney's cries. 'Tonight I got home from a night out to find him like this. I can't think what's happened.'

I had a pretty good idea, but I needed to be sure. I knelt beside him in the waiting room to give him a quick check. His abdomen was bloated and tight, and he yelped when I touched it.

'He's very bloated. I'm afraid this could be quite serious. Would you mind waiting? I'll take him straight through to the senior vets, then come back to get a fuller history from you while they start working on him.'

I ran to get a trolley to wheel Barney through to the ER. Doug helped me to lift him gently onto it and then patted him on the head. I wheeled him through the double doors and Stacy rushed over. 'He's really bloated. I think it's a twisted stomach,' I said. She checked him over, put the ultrasound probe on him to confirm the diagnosis and nodded.

'OK, he'll need surgery, but first we need to deflate his stomach; the build-up of gas is what's hurting him. Jo, you can do this.'

We clipped a small patch of fur from Barney's abdomen and applied antiseptic, then Stacy handed me a two-inch-long needle. Clenching my teeth, I plunged it straight through the clipped area and into Barney's stomach.

The whoosh of gas escaping sounded a bit like a balloon when you blow it up and then let go. Almost immediately Barney calmed down and stopped howling. I knelt and stroked his head. 'You've had a tough time, haven't you, young chap?' Barney raised his head, licked my hand and managed two thumps of his tail.

A few minutes later he was taken to a kennel in the Intensive Care Unit to be prepped for surgery while I went back, with Stacy, to talk to Doug and to take Barney's history.

'What is a twisted stomach?' he asked. 'How did it happen?'

'It's not uncommon in deep-chested breeds of dog,' I told him. 'It's a condition called gastric dilation volvulus or GDV, in which the stomach twists and dilates when it can't expel food or gas. The blood supply can also be cut off. GDV sometimes happens after a big meal followed by exercise, but frequently there isn't an obvious reason.'

'Barney always seems to be hungry,' Doug said. 'He steals anything he can get hold of; we have to keep all our food out of reach. The only things he doesn't seem to like are carrots. Yesterday he ate my son's headphones, a plate of biscuits and the insole of a boot.'

I laughed. 'That's a Lab for you. Happy dogs, but big eaters. What happened to Barney wasn't necessarily anything he ate; we still don't know all the reasons why dogs get twisted stomachs.'

I explained that we'd relieved the pressure of the build-up of gas, which could eventually have ruptured the stomach wall, and that Barney would need immediate surgery to return his stomach to the right position and to check for any other internal damage. 'He's sleeping now, we've given him pain relief and we'll give you a call as soon as he's out of surgery.'

'Thanks.' Doug smiled. 'I'll be off then. Got to get up for work at six.'

I looked at my watch. It was ten past two. Ten hours into my shift and there were still new patients coming through every few minutes.

By three things were quieter and at half-past Stacy told me I could go.

'Have you had fun?' she grinned. 'ECC can be a bit of a baptism of fire.'

'I've loved it,' I said. 'I felt like a real vet tonight.'

As I headed out to the car park the hospital's hushed corridors felt peaceful. For a brief hour or two, until the day staff began to arrive, everything was calm.

I climbed into my little Volvo C30 and drove back to the house I shared with four other vet students in the village of Welham Green, five minutes from the campus. It just so happened (honest) that the other four were boys, despite the fact that eighty per cent of students in my year were girls. But despite the teasing I'd had from some of my friends, there was strictly no romance with any of them – we all just got on really well.

The house was in darkness as I crept in through the front door and made my way into the kitchen. Even Buddy, the sixth member of our household, a funny little mutt that one of my housemates had inherited from his grandparents, barely stirred in his basket.

Despite the late – or was it early? – hour, I was still buzzing with all that I'd learned and done over the past twelve hours. I made myself a cup of tea and a piece of toast – standard post-night-out fare – and sat at the kitchen table.

Fifteen minutes later the exhaustion hit me. I crawled upstairs and was asleep within seconds.

16

CHAPTER TWO

Black Monday

Most people decide they want to be vets when they're four years old and fall in love with their hamster, or kitten, or puppy. But for me the lightbulb moment didn't come until I was sixteen. Until then I was pretty sure I wanted to be a forensic scientist – I loved the idea of solving mysteries – but when I was offered the chance to do a couple of weeks' work experience with a local veterinary practice I realised how much people love and depend on their animals, and that if we help the animal, we help the owner, whether that's an elderly person whose cat means the world to them or a farmer who depends on his cows for his income. Being a vet wasn't just about animals; it was about people, too. There was also a forensic side to it. A vet has to examine all the available information to determine what's wrong with an animal and while that's sometimes obvious, it can also be a bit of a mystery.

I was sold.

I come from a family of animal-lovers, which helps. We've always had dogs, mostly springer spaniels; affectionate, loyal and energetic dogs. By the time I went to college we'd had Tosca for about eight years and Paddy, a little Yorkshire terrier, for four. Paddy came to us after his elderly owner died and the RSPCA discovered about 200 Yorkies in a squalid, windowless shed, all of them in a dreadful condition. Some of them died and the rest were farmed out to different rescue organisations. Paddy was only eight months old when we got him, a little brown ball of hair. He seemed to have survived the ordeal pretty well and he and Tosca soon bonded, she took him under her wing and they'd snuggle on the sofa together.

We also had my two horses, Elli and Tammy. I'd been mad about horses since I was five years old, when my friend started riding lessons and I begged my parents to let me learn, too. It was a huge financial commitment for my parents, but for Mum, being around horses was an unfulfilled childhood dream, and Dad just wanted to get as far away from his city job as possible at weekends. Only my younger brother Ross didn't share the passion, having received a hoof in the groin during his first riding lesson when he was five. There was no way he was going near a horse again.

We bought Elli when I was twelve. She was a six-year-old bay, dark brown with a black mane and tail, chestnut dapples and huge dark eyes. She was my fun horse, so safe I could even ride her without a saddle. We won lots of rosettes together at local gymkhanas, but three years later she went badly lame. The vet told us she would never be a competition horse again and that she should be put down. The alternatives were to box-rest her in stables for a year or so, or to put her in a field, let her roam free and see what happened.

It was a huge blow to me. Elli was my world and there was no way I was going to let her be put to sleep. She'd always hated stables, so we chose to put her in the field and let her run loose. Two years later she was no longer lame but very unfit, so I began riding her to get her fit enough to enter competitions again.

While Elli was recovering I got Tammy, a four-year-old bay whose broad brown flanks have an orange glow in the sun. Tammy was much more highly strung than Elli. Nervous around other horses, she would bare her teeth if she got scared, but she was willing and bold and she learned new tricks really fast.

Tammy was so unpredictable that at competitions she would either come first or be disqualified after terrifying the audience by rearing or trashing the jumps. I was never scared with her because I'd been around horses for ten years when I got her, and I had a Saturday job in which I trained difficult and young horses. I also had a bum like glue, so I seldom fell off her, even when she was misbehaving. Elli became the one horse Tammy trusted, and by the time I left for college Tammy and Elli were sharing a field at the stables up the road from us and were happy in one another's company. I knew I'd miss them dreadfully, but I planned to get home as often as possible, and I arranged to loan them out to other riders so that they'd be exercised.

Once I decided that I wanted to be a vet there was no stopping me. I worked incredibly hard to make the A-level grades I needed, and Dad and I went to look around potential vet schools.

There were seven veterinary colleges I could apply to (there are eight now), but the moment I saw it my heart was set on the Royal Veterinary College. With two campuses, in Camden and Hertfordshire, it has fantastic teaching facilities, including the Queen Mother Hospital for Animals, its own Equine Centre and its own first-opinion practice. So I was heartbroken when they turned me down. I decided to call them and find out why, and when I was told it was because I didn't have physics GCSE I told them that there had been a mistake, because I did have it. I begged for an interview, but they said the interviews were almost over. Eventually they relented and said I could come on the last day of interviews, for the final appointment of the day.

I did and I was accepted. But as I was right at the end of the interviews, all the places had already been allocated for that September and so I was offered one for the following year. That was fine with me; I was prepared to wait and I decided to spend my gap year working and travelling.

A year later, when I walked through the doors of the RVC's Camden campus to start my course, I felt ready to take on whatever the college was going to throw at me over the next five years. I knew that by the end I would need to know how to do everything – diagnosis, treatment and surgery – on any animal at any time, anywhere, from a well-equipped surgery to a grubby barn, and I couldn't wait to get going.

For the first two years we were based in Camden before transferring to the Hawkshead campus in Potters Bar, Hertfordshire, for the final three years. And until the spring term of our fourth year everything went smoothly. My days were filled with lectures, essays and studying dry bones, specimens in bottles, X-rays, plastic models and charts. Everything, in fact, but live animal cases.

We knew that was coming, of course, but it didn't seem real until, one bleak January day in 2013, all 250 of us in the year group were gathered together in the lecture theatre by our Vice Principal, David Church, a charismatic Australian who was passionate about getting the best out of his students. He was a genius, and incredibly intimidating for that reason, but we'd come to realise that ultimately he was on our side and always put the health and welfare of the students above everything else.

That January morning he looked around the auditorium at a sea of expectant faces. 'This is the start of the rest of your lives. It's time to put everything you've learned into practice,' he announced. 'You're going to go out there and be vets, and you'll be expected to know your stuff and get it right. You're not students now, you're colleagues of the vets you'll be working with, part of the team, and you'll be expected to know what to do.'

I was sitting to one side of the lecture theatre with my housemates, Andrew, James, Kevin and John, plus James's girlfriend Hannah, who was a semi-permanent fixture in our house. Lucy was in the row behind. We always chose a spot well out of David Church's direct eye line because he tended to pick on students and ask them alarming questions.

I turned to Lucy. 'Are you feeling as nervous as I am?' I whispered.

'More,' she replied. 'I'm actually about to be sick.'

I looked over at the boys. Andrew looked cool and calm. He never seemed to get excited or nervous about anything, and was incredibly steady. Kevin looked worried and James even more so, but John looked excited. He couldn't wait to get stuck in.

The five of us couldn't have been more different. Goodness knows how we ended up sharing a house together, but after a year in student accommodation we'd opted to move into a small house in Camden in our second year, and we'd decided to stay together when we moved to Hertfordshire in our third. We'd been lucky with the house we found as the owners were going abroad and, amazingly, didn't mind letting to students.

Being the only girl I'd bagged the best room. But for the boys the room that mattered was the kitchen, and this one had two ovens and six hobs. Food wasn't a priority for me. I tried to keep my food budget to £10 a week and ate whatever was on offer at the supermarket so that I could save for other things, but the four boys were all big eaters.

James loved to cook and had an entire rack of spices. At weekends you'd find him creating gourmet dishes like pulled pork and fennel or Thai green curry to share with Hannah. He had a slow cooker and would put a casserole on in the morning to be ready for when he came back in the evening.

Andrew was stick thin but could pile away more food than anyone I'd ever seen; he liked substantial dishes like spaghetti with meatballs or big roasts. He'd eat a huge plateful and be back for more two hours later.

Kevin and John were both from the States, but that was all they had in common. Kevin was from South Carolina and was an outdoor, baseball and hiking kind of guy who loved his steak, burger and fries. Top of his list was grits, or ground corn; it was his staple diet and he'd bring back bags of the stuff every time he went to the States. We all thought it was just like Italian polenta that you can get in a lot of supermarkets, but Kevin insisted that they weren't the same at all and he had to have the authentic Yankee version from home.

Every Halloween his parents would send over a bulk order of candy corn, which tastes like fudge, comes in the shape of sweetcorn and is orange and white. We loved it and dug into the huge jar every time we passed.

While Kevin missed the wide open spaces of America, John was a city guy from New York. Neat, clean and organised, he kept his room pristine and tidied up after all of us. John loved English culture, he thought the English were terribly polite and he loved traditions like afternoon tea. He shipped his Mini Cooper over from the States because he didn't want to drive any other car, and he liked to make himself fancy dishes like chicken salad with pomegranate seeds and feta. He also made bread, enough for all of us, and on the days when I had no time or money for anything else his fresh bread kept me going.

All the boys were in different groups and on a different rotation schedule to mine, so I was grateful for Lucy. An hour after David Church's talk we sat in the canteen, going through our rotations timetables. Altogether we would be going through sixteen different core rotations, some a week long, some two weeks. The essential ones would include farm animal medicine, first-opinion practice (which means being part of a local veterinary practice), equine medicine, and specialist areas such as neurology, surgery, anaesthesia and orthopaedics. In addition we would have three fortnights in which we could choose our own rotation electives, and sixteen weeks in which we were expected to carry out work experience, which we had to set up ourselves. We'd started writing to practices months earlier, asking if they would accept us for work experience, which had to fit into the gaps between the required college rotations. It was enough to make the most confident student's head spin.

'Horses first,' I said. 'That's good for me.'

'Not me,' Lucy said gloomily. 'I'm not keen on horses. I prefer cows, so give me a cowshed over a stable anytime.'

'I'll watch your back with the horses if you watch mine with the cows.'

She grinned. 'Deal.'

Lucy and I were close, and there wasn't much we didn't tell each other. We had a lot of interests in common; we were both musical and also sporty, outdoor people. We played a lot of tennis together, but when it came to running our paths diverged; Lucy ran marathons while I was happy to settle for a mile or two with the dog.

Thank goodness we'd got into the same rotation group. I didn't know the other three girls on our rotation – Grace, Jade and Katy – but soon after we'd been given our groups at the end of the autumn term, Lucy and I met Grace at the Christmas Ball. She bounced up, put an arm round each of us and said merrily, 'Hello, girls, I think we're going to be working together.'

Lucy and I laughed. 'Nice to meet you, too. See you on Black Monday.'

'Yup,' Grace called, as her boyfriend Miles led her away, 'it's going to be a laugh.'

Black Monday was the first day of rotations. So-called, no doubt, because it was the day on which every single student was filled with unmitigated terror.

For us it fell on a bitterly cold day in early February, when the five of us gathered at 8am by the whiteboard in the RVC's Equine Hospital, ready to begin large animal imaging, all of us pale with lack of sleep and visibly nervous. Grace, in total contrast to her appearance at the ball, was jittery and anxious. 'Not good with horses,' she muttered.

Jade had a bit of experience with horses but none of the others did, so I felt lucky. But liking horses and knowing how to treat them were two different things, and I'd spent the previous weekend cramming over my textbooks, trying to memorise every possible horse complaint.

For equine work we all had to wear green overalls with our name tags pinned to the front. Rumour had it that if you forgot your name tag you failed the rotation. I wasn't absolutely sure that this was true, but just to be safe I'd had mine within sight all weekend. Underneath the overalls I had a thick fleece and, like the others, I was wearing sturdy boots padded out with warm socks.

The Equine Hospital was part of the Large Animal Clinical Centre. We'd been into the barn around the back during training, but until now we'd never entered the hallowed portals of the main building, which was a working hospital open to the public. Before starting we were given a tour by one of the more junior vets. It was an impressive place, with consultation rooms, an imaging centre offering bone-scanning, MRI, CT and X-rays, two surgical theatres, and three stable blocks, one of them the Intensive Care Unit. We would be back here again later in the year for equine medicine, surgery and orthopaedics, but this time our focus was the imaging suite.

Everything in it was large scale. It had to be. And, as we quickly discovered, imaging a horse was no mean feat. To take a CT (computerised tomography) scan, a human would be asked to lie on a flat bed while an X-ray tube rotates around their body. With horses, only the head and neck fit in the tube, so if any other part of the body needs to be imaged a standard X-ray has to be taken. The machine is suspended from the ceiling, with handles either side, while the radiographer moves it around the room like a submarine scope. It can be positioned anywhere around the horse, while someone holds a receptor plate on the end of a long wooden pole on the other side. Not easy, and it gets more complicated than that, because the angles have to be right so that the horse's bones don't get superimposed over each other.

Kitted up in lead gowns and gloves to protect us from the X-rays, we spent a lot of time learning the right angles to use, and then running out of the room while the image was taken (all bar the lucky two holding the horse and the plate) and back in again.

But our first job that grey February morning was to assist with bone-scanning, or to give it its technical name, scintigraphy, on a large grey Arab stallion. The clinician in charge that day was Jackie. In her mid-thirties and very friendly, she was aware of how nervous we all were and went out of her way to help us and make sure we were enjoying ourselves as well as learning.

The Arab stallion was lame, but there was no obvious reason why. Hence the bone scan, which is a good way of locating where the problem is when it's not immediately obvious. Before the scan the horse is given an intravenous injection of a radioactive substance that spreads around its body, binding to areas where the bone is trying to heal itself and emitting radioactive rays that show up on the scans.

As one of the others stood holding the heavily sedated horse and stroking its nose, the scanner was moved around it, section by section. And, as we discovered, it takes absolutely ages. It's not unusual to spend four hours scanning a horse, so we were taking it in shifts, holding the horse, observing the scans with the clinician or doing the other vital job – catching the horse's radioactive pee in a bucket.

I was the lucky candidate first up for this job so, bucket in hand, I hovered around the horse's rear end. I felt pretty silly and, to make matters worse, Lucy, who was holding the horse, kept catching my eye and making me laugh. As I lunged forward, just a moment too late to stop another waterfall of radioactive pee hitting the floor, Lucy snorted with laughter. 'Just wait till it's your turn,' I mouthed at her.

It seemed like an age until we finished, but the end result showed that the horse had an inflammation in the pelvis. The only treatment, as Jackie the clinician explained, was rest and pain relief.

Over a brief lunch we chatted to the other three in our group. Now that we were underway, Grace had begun to get a little of her bounce back. Katy was quiet, but prone to cracking wicked jokes. And Jade was funny and very upfront – she said what she thought. They were all lovely, but I did wonder if, as we were going to be together so much, personality clashes would emerge.

Lucy and Jade were both trying out online dating, which led to a lot of laughter and discussion along the lines of, 'Oh, look at him, what do you think? No, he's definitely not my type, what about this one? That one looks like one of the horses, but here, take a look, this one's quite hot.'

Grace, Katy and I weren't in the market for dates, so we provided second opinions and back-up. Grace was living with her boyfriend, Miles, Katy wasn't looking for a relationship and I had Jacques, the lovely South African I'd met during my gap year. By then we'd been dating long-distance for almost four years. We used Skype and our phones to stay in touch, but I missed him.

Apart from the horse pee/bucket challenge, things appeared to be pretty straightforward so far, but that afternoon we faced a much bigger test. An X-ray on the hock (the joint in the middle of the back leg) of a lame horse showed that a lot of things were wrong. This horse was elderly and the hock showed little bone protrusions, erosion, swelling and ankylosis, or bone fusion.

We had to stand round the X-ray and point out to Jackie what we saw, taking it in turns to come up with new things. This was a scene we would be repeating many times throughout rotations, in which students sweated and panicked, and clinicians looked patiently (or impatiently in a lot of cases) at them waiting for answers. If the person before you said the thing you had planned to say, you just had to come up with something else. The clinicians were never satisfied until they had squeezed multiple answers out of each of us.

Once we'd exhausted the list of visible irregularities, Jackie asked whether we thought the ankylosis was hurting the horse. My horse Elli had been through this, so I knew that once fused the bones in the two immobile hock joints no longer hurt because they had stopped moving. Feeling a touch smug, since everyone else had said yes, I said no, and was rewarded with a 'Well done' from Jackie, and 'Just wait till we get to the cows' and a wink from Lucy.

Next up was Honey, a lovely bay with a back problem. She had become unhappy with being ridden and an X-ray revealed that she had kissing spine; two of her vertebrae were touching each other, which must have been very painful for her. Luckily kissing spine is easy to treat; Honey would go for surgery, which could be done under local anaesthetic, and until then she'd be given pain relief via powder in her food.

By the end of the ten-hour day we were exhausted. Heady with relief that we'd made it through Black Monday, we raced each other around the imaging suite in the chairs on wheels, there for the infinitely more serious purpose of allowing clinicians to move around the horse while holding the scanner, but great for a little light relief before heading home.

Back at the house Andrew was cooking up a cauldron of pasta after his day in the QMH working on small animal imaging. Kevin, John and James were all away on their rotations.

'How was your first day?' I asked.

'It was all right. Got pretty badly grilled over an X-ray image, though. They asked if it was an image from a dog or a cat. Surely I would know if I've just X-rayed a dog or a cat and I wouldn't need to work it out from an image.'

'So you couldn't tell?'

'Er, no.'

I laughed. Then it dawned on me I had no idea myself. 'So when I get asked that question next week on small animal imaging, how exactly do I tell if it's a dog or a cat?'

He looked at me and sighed, then went back to stirring the pasta. 'You look at the vertebrae. Cats' are long, dogs' are short. Also the femur. Cats' are straight, dogs' are slightly curved.'

'Thanks, appreciate it.'

I was grateful for the tip – at least that was one mistake I hoped to avoid. After four years of study there were still so many things to get wrong. Things we'd only realise we didn't know when some gimlet-eyed senior vet put us on the spot. I could feel my cheeks burn just thinking about it.

I hated messing up, but I was already beginning to realise that if the system of rotations was about anything, it was about making mistakes and then learning how to get it right, so that once we were let loose on the world as qualified vets we would know what we were doing.

I stuck a couple of pieces of cheese toast under the grill and went to Skype Jacques. At the end of March I would be heading to South Africa to see him and to do some work experience in the sun, and I couldn't wait. Only six weeks to go. Six weeks of hard graft, endless grilling and a lot of wet noses.

CHAPTER THREE

The Vaccine Trick and Dermaholiday

Sometimes the simplest things give you the biggest head-aches. Like administering kennel cough vaccine – something vets have to do all the time.

It should be so easy. You prepare the vaccine and then squirt it up the dog's nose. And that would be fine, if it wasn't for the snorting, sneezing, head-shaking canines determined to get it all out again.

I looked at the young retriever sniffing round the surgery, tail wagging enthusiastically.

'Let's put Jiffy up on the table, shall we?' I said to the owner, who was dressed in a smart navy suit.

Once on the examining table, as his owner stood next to me, I held Jiffy's head up, positioned the plunger and squirted – just as Jiffy jerked out of my grip, shook his head and snorted the vaccine all over his owner's face and the front of her jacket.

'What was that?' she asked, startled.

'I'm so sorry, it's some of the vaccine, but don't worry, it's not toxic and it shouldn't stain. Let me get you a tissue.' My cheeks were scarlet.

As she mopped the vaccine off her face and clothes I could only hope that some of it had actually got into the dog it was intended for. And I made a mental note – always position the owner behind the dog.

I was on a fortnight's work experience in a small, friendly veterinary practice close to my family home in Kent. It was a great opportunity for me to get some hands-on experience, with the added bonus of being able to see a bit of my family in the evenings.

This placement was one I'd arranged myself, as part of the sixteen weeks of EMS – Extra-Mural Studies – that we were expected to fit in between the compulsory rotations allocated by the college.

Puddlefoot is a country practice based in a building that looks a bit like a mobile home, but bigger. The staff I was working with included four friendly vets, a couple of them part-time, and a very helpful and chatty nurse, Chloe. The patients we saw were ninety-five per cent small animals, plus a few horses. The vets were encouraging and helpful, and with their supervision they allowed me to do consultations, give injections, scrub in to help during surgery and administer vaccines – hence the embarrassing scene with Jiffy and his owner.

That wasn't my only vaccine disaster, either. My next patient was a tiny eight-week-old Chihuahua, a fluffy little ball with the minutest nose I'd ever seen. I took one look at it and my heart sank. No way was I going to get the whole vial of kennel cough vaccine into that nose. I drew up the vaccine into the syringe, and the dog started shaking its head before I'd even approached. All I could do, as I placed the syringe in front of one minuscule nostril, was hope that a bit would go in and that the owner, a charming elderly woman whom I positioned carefully behind her dog, wouldn't notice how much of it dripped down the dog's face and was snorted onto both me and the table.

As a final-year student I was being taught about the latest developments in the industry, and the practice vets were keen to know what I could pass on. When a cheerful collie came in with urinary incontinence, it was a chance to show off my knowledge because we'd done it as a topic just a few weeks earlier. The vets liked quizzing me on subjects, not only to help me reinforce what I had been learning but also to remind themselves. One of the vets, Cheryl, started asking me about the modes of action of different drugs that work on the bladder, so I drew a bladder on the white-board, with all the drug receptors. 'It's been years since I've gone into this much detail,' Cheryl laughed. 'It's great to have a refresher.'

Most of the time I was the novice learning from everyone else, so it felt good to be able to redress the balance a bit.

The funniest case that week was a beautiful, glossy saluki crossbreed called Matilda, who had torn her ear on a barbed-wire fence. Ears bleed and bleed, and when their ears feel funny, dogs shake their heads. Matilda soon had the surgery looking like something out of a horror film, as her ear flapped from side to side, spattering blood up the walls and all over everyone in the room.

We treated the wound with cauterising powder and bandaged the ear to her head like a helmet. Then off she went, with her very charming owners, a young mum called Tina and her five-year-old daughter, Daisy, who giggled non-stop as we bandaged Matilda's head.

'You know, Daisy,' I said, 'at university they teach us to bandage on cuddly toys, so I've fixed the ear of many squishy doggies with poorly ears.' Daisy giggled even more.

A couple of days later they were back for a change of bandage, along with Daisy's cuddly-toy puppy, who now had a heavily bandaged head, which I duly admired.

The moment the bandage was removed, Matilda shook her head, opened up the wound again and redecorated the surgery with what seemed to be another litre or two of blood. We all sighed, cauterised the wound again and re-bandaged the ear, before wiping down the consulting room before the next client came in.

After the third time this happened, Tina was getting worried. 'Is it ever going to heal?' she said. 'We seem to be going round in circles.'

We did, and although the ear wasn't hurting Matilda too much, we needed it to stop bleeding. Once again, under Cheryl's watchful eye, I bandaged it up, making Matilda look like a one-eared alien. 'This time we'll take our chances and leave it for an extra day or two,' Cheryl said firmly. 'The issue's not that it isn't healing. It's healing pretty well, but every time we take off the bandage Matilda opens it up again. Next time she comes in, after the extra couple of days, it will hopefully have had time to heal a bit more and won't reopen. But since there are risks to leaving a bandage on, if it starts to smell or you see anything soaking through, bring her back in straight away and we'll have to come up with a plan B.' We all gave a sigh of relief.

At the end of each day I drove back to my family home near Tunbridge Wells. We had lived in the same house since I was one, and I always loved going back to a proper meal and my own bed. Ross was away at university, so it was just me, my mum Clare, my dad Giles and the dogs, Paddy and Tosca. I'm close to my parents – we've always enjoyed each other's company – so it was nice to catch up with them and fill them in on how the rotations were going. Each evening, Mum cooked my favourite beef stew or shepherd's pie, and it was a rare treat to relax in front of the television with the dogs.

We're all animal lovers and Mum was juggling her Open University degree in Humanities with Creative Writing with her other passion, working as a volunteer transporting rescue dogs to new homes. After we got Paddy, Mum realised that a dog being cared for by an animal charity is often miles away from the people willing to give it a home. A network of willing volunteers with transport is vital. Mum would get a call, often at short notice, asking her to collect a dog and deliver it to the new owners, or in cases where the dog needed to travel long distances, to be part of a team collecting the dog from the previous driver and taking it on to the next. The transport charity she helped out did much more than just delivering dogs from charities to new homes, though. It also picked up dogs from pounds when their time was up and they were about to be put to sleep, and took them to charities that would provide them with training, which would mean they could be put up for adoption. She was helping to save lives.

After my two weeks with the team at Puddlefoot, I packed my bags and headed back to the Queen Mother Hospital for dermatology, known by the students as 'dermaholiday' because it involved cushy hours, no emergencies and straightforward consultations, generally along the lines of 'How long has your dog/cat been scratching?'

Dermatology is mostly about allergies, and a big part of the job is persuading the owners that they need to take the allergies seriously. A lot end up at the QMH with their dogs and cats because they've ignored the advice of their first-opinion vet and continued to feed Tibbles or Rover food that is making them itch and break out in rashes. Eventually either they demand a second opinion or their exasperated vet suggests they see a specialist.

The only real way to find out what's causing the allergy, once you've ruled out parasites like fleas and mites, is by a process of elimination. The animal has to change to a hypo-allergenic food for six weeks to see if the problem clears up. If it does, after that you can gently re-introduce other foods, watching to see if there's any reaction. If the food elimination doesn't work, you can assume it's an environmental allergy and start the process of trying to desensitise the animal, although in many cases it's down to food and eliminating the allergen should be all that's needed.

But for some owners it isn't quite so straightforward. Take the very earnest lady, Mrs Hooper, who came in with her little pug dog, Muffin. A blood test had indicated that Muffin, who was scratching and rubbing his head on the floor, was definitely allergic but, as is often the case, the test hadn't indicated what he was specifically allergic to. It only indicated he was allergic to a great number of things.

'Start with his food,' I explained to Mrs Hooper, under the watchful eye of the dermatology clinician, Annie. 'Give him hypo-allergenic food and nothing else for six weeks, and see whether his condition improves.'

'Oh, I've done that,' Mrs H said. 'It didn't help.'

'Are you certain that was all he had?'

'Yes. Well, apart from his chews, but they're chicken and chicken's good for sick dogs, isn't it?'

'Well, it can be. Chicken is plain so it can be good for a dog with stomach problems. But in some cases it can actually be the problem. Plenty of dogs are allergic to chicken.'

'No, it isn't that because he was still scratching when he was eating beef chunks.'

'I'm afraid that nearly all processed dog food, even beef chunks, has chicken in it. The company only has to have a certain percentage of beef in the food to be able to call it beef chunks, and the remainder is made up of other meat. So you really do need to give him the hypo-allergenic food on its own and nothing else. At all. No biscuits, chews or treats of any kind.'

Mrs H looked put out. 'Well, that seems a bit hard on him. He really does love his treats.'

I tried to sound patient. 'I know it's hard, I really do appreciate that. And I'm sure he loves his treats. What dog doesn't? But put yourself in Muffin's shoes. Would you want to be itchy and uncomfortable all the time? You can always give him the hypo-allergenic food as treats, too. If the allergy isn't cleared up it may lead to ear infections, bald patches and sore spots on his skin. So it's really worth giving it a good go.'

Silence.

'Oh. Well. All right then. If you insist.'

This conversation, or a version of it, happened a couple of times a day and was no doubt a re-run of the conversation the pet owner's own vet had already had with them. Often it was only because a specialist repeated the advice that the owner eventually acted on it.

Of course, not all pet allergies are due to food; pets can also be allergic to dust-mites, fleas and pollen, which can make life for their owners pretty difficult. But food is always the place to start, and with the majority of pets this is where the answer lies.

One afternoon while I was in the dermatology unit a deafening alarm went off. 'Crash,' shouted Annie as she sprinted out of the room.

I went to the door, to see an impressively athletic clinician race past me, hurdle a trolley that someone had left across the corridor and disappear in the direction of the Intensive Care Unit.

'What on earth is going on? Where has Annie gone?' I asked.

'It's the crash alarm. My housemates told me about this,' Lucy replied, joining me in the doorway as we watched more clinicians sprinting down the corridor. Lucy had spent the previous year living with three girls in the year above us, so she was invaluable when it came to hints and tips about rotations. 'The alarm goes when an animal suddenly needs resuscitating or serious emergency care. Usually the case is either in the ICU or in surgery, and all members of staff who are available to drop what they're doing have to run to help.'

'I wish we could help,' I said.

At that moment, an intern turned the corner into our corridor coming back from the direction in which clinicians had been sprinting minutes earlier.

'What's going on?' Lucy called to him, eager to be filled in on the story.

'We had a cocker spaniel in ICU, whose heart stopped. The clinicians who got there before me had the defibrillators and adrenaline out and they'd intubated it. They were doing all they could. Luckily lots of people were available, and so the ICU was pretty crowded. I was just in the way, so I left. Unfortunately it doesn't look good, though.'

Half an hour later Annie was back. 'We lost it,' she said. 'Lovely little dog, but it had septic peritonitis. That's such a serious condition, and it threw its heart into a fatal arrhythmia. Its heart just couldn't cope.'

I felt terribly sad. Someone had just lost a beloved pet, and it reminded me how close my family had come to losing our dog, Tosca, when she had the same condition just over a year earlier.

It had all started when Tosca began acting very strangely. Instead of being her normal annoying self and constantly demanding attention, she started hiding in strange places around the house and we'd end up hunting for her.

This went on for a few weeks until, one Saturday evening when I was at home for the weekend, I found her lying on her side groaning, with the biggest belly I had ever seen. She had managed to get into her dry food sack and eat an enormous amount before drinking a whole bowl of water. This was strange behaviour. She'd always loved her food and been a bit of a scavenger, but she'd never stolen from her food sack before.

Tosca had eaten so much that I felt alarmed. I rushed her to our local out-of-hours vet, Louise, who decided that there was too much food in her stomach for it to pass, because it had swollen with the water. Tosca would need to go into surgery that night so that her stomach could be opened and the food removed. Louise promised to call us when it was all over.

I spent the night in a restless doze, waiting for the call to say she was out of surgery and had come round from the anaesthetic. But it never came.

By two in the morning, four hours after I'd left her, I decided to call and see what was taking so long. Louise explained the surgery had gone well, but Tosca wasn't waking up from the anaesthetic smoothly. She had been waiting for Tosca to wake fully before phoning.

By morning Tosca had finally woken up, but she was in a critical condition and clearly very ill. It was a Sunday, and I had to travel back to university. My parents promised to let me know how Tosca was, and I drove back feeling very afraid that something more than just a food-gorging incident might be going on.

On Monday afternoon Mum phoned. Tosca was deteriorating and she had been referred as an emergency to the Queen Mother Hospital. Mum was driving her up immediately, collecting Dad from his train on the way.

I waited outside the hospital as my parents drove into the car park, then ran over to open the boot of the car. Tosca was such a sorry sight. I was used to a bouncy, full-of-life dog, who would normally be leaping up to lick my face in greeting. But now she remained limp and unresponsive. Attached to an intravenous drip, she couldn't even stand up.

Gently I lifted her in my arms and took her into the hospital, where the receptionist phoned the emergency team. Seconds later several vets and nurses rushed out with a trolley to whisk her away.

After giving an account of Tosca's history to an impressively thorough final-year student, a tense hour passed before we were called into a consulting room with the senior clinician, Giacomo. Little was I to know that he would be the clinician in charge when I would be doing my ECC rotation a year later. He explained that Tosca's abdomen had become septic after her operation and as a consequence her heart had started beating in an irregular rhythm that could be fatal. Even with further surgery to flush out the infected fluid, together with medication for her heart, she would only have a fifty-fifty chance.

I could feel the sob rising in my throat. Tosca was an invincible dog. And she was only ten, not old for a spaniel. How could this be happening? The clinician gave us a moment and then asked gently that if Tosca were to crash, should she be resuscitated? We said yes, of course, but desperately hoped it wouldn't come to that.

He took us through to give Tosca a cuddle. I stroked her head and those floppy, silky ears, praying that it wouldn't be the last time I saw her. Tosca was taken to surgery, my parents drove home and I went back to Welham Green to wait.

Once again there was no phone call. Hours passed as I tried to tell myself that no news was good news. Four in the morning came and went and I was still wide awake, so eventually I gave in and phoned. Tosca had made it through surgery, but was still in a critical condition. She hadn't come round from the anaesthetic as expected, which could be indicative of a brain tumour – and this would also explain her recent change in behaviour. In addition, they had found another small cancerous tumour on her adrenal gland, but it was so close to a blood vessel that it couldn't be safely removed.

The news that she had cancer as well as septic peritonitis was pretty devastating, but there was still hope. The cancer was in its early stages and might be a slow-growing type, so there was a good chance that she would have another couple of years if she made it through this ordeal. I said a little prayer. 'Come on, Tosca,' I whispered. 'Don't give up now.'

First thing the next morning I went in to visit her. She was in the Intensive Care Unit and I had to battle through a jungle of wires and tubes just to get to her. She had two fluid lines going into her, a urinary catheter, a drain out of her abdomen and four ECG wires. The ICU unit, surprisingly, was a very calm room, full of composed, friendly and helpful clinicians and nurses.

A week later Tosca was still in the ICU. Her heart had regained its normal rhythm, but she wasn't recovering as fast as she should. She was very depressed and not eating, which was so unlike her. The staff decided that maybe a change of scenery would help, so she was moved to the much brighter soft-tissue ward. Another day passed, and she was much the same, so they took a further sample of fluid from her abdomen. The culture showed that she had a very resistant strain of bacteria that wasn't responding to the antibiotics she was on. It was a testament to her strength that she'd made it this far.

Tosca was put on one of the strongest antibiotic drugs available, and over the next few days she gradually began to improve. As a vet student I was allowed to visit often, and I spent hours every day sitting in her kennel giving her cuddles, catching up on my studies and talking to final-year vet students about their experience of being on rotations. Tosca was still refusing food, and she had lost an alarming amount of weight. The ICU nurses tried to entice her to eat, and I tried, too, but she refused everything until, after eight days, when the clinicians were starting to seriously consider placing a feeding tube in her under anaesthetic, she finally let me give her a small piece of sausage. I joked that she must have heard that if she didn't eat she would need to have another procedure.

After three weeks she was finally well enough to go home. It was a Friday, which was great, as it meant I could travel back with her. My parents met me at the hospital and Tosca was brought out, still weak and wobbly, but with a wag in her tail. Mum and Dad had tears in their eyes; we all adored Tosca and we had come so close to losing her.

We put her on her bed in the boot of the car for the two-hour journey home. Soon after pulling out of the car park, Tosca started howling and yapping. It was a habit that she had when she was excited or wanted to go for a walk. Normally it annoyed us, but now the sound of her yaps was like sweet music. We all laughed. We had our Tosca back.

Over the following months Tosca recovered well, but then she gradually lost her sight and her head began to tilt to the left, confirming that a slow-growing brain tumour was probably the root cause of her problems. But even blind she coped remarkably well. She knew the layout of the house and she still insisted on charging around as she always had. Since trying to slow her down was an impossible task, we put bubble wrap around the trees in the garden and horse boots on the legs of the dining room chairs. She had no problem finding us and then, as she always had, sitting at our feet and pawing at our laps until we gave her our undivided attention. And her radar still guided her unerringly towards the dishwasher after dinner, where she licked the plates as it was being loaded.

We were lucky with Tosca. It could so easily have gone the other way for her, but she'd survived and, a year on, she was still doing well.

Before I left dermatology for my next placement we were told that our student year group had been approached by ITN Productions, who were casting for a series about trainee vets that would be broadcast on the BBC. We were all invited to a question and answer session in which they explained that any student could apply, and that they would then pick up to ten for a reality series, following us through our final year of training.

Around a hundred students went along to the casting sessions. I decided to apply because, well, what was there to lose? And I was curious – what would it be like to be filmed? I once dreamed of being an actress, and as a child I even went to weekend stage school. Now this was the nearest I was likely to get, so I decided to have a go. At the session the producers chatted to us for a bit, and then each of us had to spend a minute talking to camera about ourselves. I thought a minute was going to seem like forever, but it went too quickly, and afterwards I left feeling that I hadn't said most of what I'd planned to say.

I didn't have time to think about it for long because the following day I packed my bags again and headed off to Wales for a fortnight of farm work. This time the five of us in my rotation group were working with another group, so there were ten of us staying together in a rented cottage. We were there to do what's known as population work – studying herds of cows on local farms and writing reports on how to improve the standard of health in each herd. We had to score every cow on nutrition, locomotion and general health, so it was pretty repetitive work.

The days when James Herriot dashed out to save the life of an ailing cow have given way to economically tougher times, as farmers, who often struggle to make a profit, can't afford to be sentimental or have one sick cow affect the health of a herd. The emphasis has to be on keeping the whole herd as healthy as possible.

With ten of us under one roof, tensions began to run high in the student house. Some of us wanted to write our reports as we went along, others wanted to leave it to the last minute, so there were a few clashes.

To escape the strains within the house – and the endless cows – Lucy and I went out to explore the area with Chloe, a friend from the other group. We drove to the Brecon Beacons, and decided to stop and walk up a hill that we were passing.

'Won't take long,' Lucy said cheerfully. 'It's only a little hill. The fresh air will do us good.'

An hour later we were working up a fair sweat as we climbed. Somehow the 'little hill' had become more of a mountain, but having decided to climb it none of us was going to be the first to turn back. By the time we got to the top we were hot, thirsty and exhausted. We sat on the grass, admiring the wild ponies and stunning views.

'See? It was worth it,' Lucy said, taking a swig of water and passing me the bottle. 'And going down will be a doddle.'

I was examining the large blister on my heel. 'Lucy,' I said, smiling sweetly, 'next time you see a "small hill" and decide to climb it, count me out.'

Soon after we got back to college at the end of the fortnight we heard that ITN had picked the first five or six students for the series. We were all agog to know who had been chosen, and were delighted to hear that one of them was Grace. She was stunned. It was going to mean working with a film crew trailing behind her at some of her trickiest moments, so she wasn't sure whether to be pleased or horrified.

I heard that I'd been put on a list of students they were undecided about. I was pretty sure that meant it would probably never happen, and that was fine with me. I had plenty to occupy me over the coming weeks and felt relieved that I wouldn't have a camera crew there to add to my embarrassment by recording the inevitable trail of blunders I'd be leaving in my wake.

CHAPTER FOUR

'Don't Cry, Englishman'

As I stepped out of the airport terminal the warm night air and the sweet, delicate scent of the ganna bushes enveloped me, and the unmistakeable chirruping of cicadas, the sound of Africa, filled my ears.

Fourteen hours earlier I had left a cold, grey London behind me and set off for Port Elizabeth in the Eastern Cape of South Africa. We flew via Johannesburg, where I changed planes for the final leg. As we began our descent I forgot about my stiff shoulders and cramped legs, and began to feel more and more excited. I hadn't seen Jacques since he'd visited me at Christmas, and it felt like an age.

He was waiting for me in the arrivals area. At six-foot-six he was impossible to miss. As I waited impatiently for my bag to arrive on the carousel we grinned at each other through the window. Mine always seemed to be the last bag to arrive ... But then I was in his arms for the warmest of hugs. He grabbed my bags and we headed out to the truck, where Jacques presented me with a beautiful bunch of lilies. He always brought me flowers, and he always left them in the car, just in case I didn't like them – as if I wouldn't!

We drove out of Port Elizabeth and onto the highway to Port Alfred, chatting away as if it had been days, rather than three months, that we had been apart. A few miles before Port Alfred Jacques swung off the main road and onto a dirt track that led twenty miles up to the old game lodge at Madolos, on the edge of a large game reserve, where Jacques lived and worked. As always, Jacques drove his Ford Ranger down the dirt road at 60 mph, kicking up clouds of red dust behind us.

The lodge was huge; Jacques lived in one wing and the other was for his students. He taught at a university that offered degrees in tourism, and the lodge was the campus for the wildlife module. Students would arrive for a nine-week course in wildlife management and conservation taught by Jacques and his assistant Bongani, and they would be looked after by three large and warm-hearted ladies, Helezin, Patricia and Valencia, who cleaned and cooked, while the gardener, Michael, looked after the grounds.

When there were no students it was just Jacques rattling around in the lodge, but he didn't mind as he loved the peace and the company of the wildlife in the neighbouring reserve prowling past the garden. It wasn't unusual to see cheetahs or elephants wandering past the fence, only yards from the lodge.

Jacques and I had been together for almost four years and we'd known each other for five – ever since I went to South Africa in my gap year. I'd been nineteen, and after six months working in a livery yard to earn some money I'd booked the cheapest gap year trip I could find – three weeks doing conservation work on a game reserve in South Africa.

It was April 2009 and I spent an incredibly happy three weeks as part of a group putting up fences, cutting down trees and clearing patches of bush. Jacques, who was twenty-three, was one of the staff at the reserve who helped manage the volunteers. His job was to make us feel welcome and, when we weren't working, to take us on game drives and into town and teach us a bit about wildlife. I had lots to learn; I had no idea what an impala was (it's a species of antelope) or a sable (another species of antelope) or indeed even a springbok (yes, yet another species of antelope) and I soaked up all the new information.

Jacques and I got on from the start. He's broad, muscular and, with his height, he can appear intimidating, but he's actually a big softie and very easy to talk to. We became good friends and along with the other volunteers, who were a really nice bunch, we had a lot of fun.

When I got back home I missed South Africa, so when Jacques got in touch a couple of weeks later to say that he and his friend Daniel were taking a trip up to Kruger National Park and would I like to come along, I didn't hesitate. I blew my savings on a ticket and six weeks later I returned. One of the other volunteers, an American girl called Abby, had been travelling round Europe and Jacques invited her, too.

South Africa is enormous, many times bigger than the UK, and people there drive huge distances without even thinking about it. Johannesburg is a fifteen-hour drive from the reserve where Jacques was living. He and Daniel drove up to meet us at the airport and then we drove for another four or five hours up to Kruger National Park in the north east. One of the largest game reserves in Africa, Kruger covers over 7,500 square miles. Abby and I had the perfect companions as Jacques and Daniel were both qualified guides, and we spent two weeks watching the game and the extraordinary landscape. We ate rusks and drank coffee for breakfast, drove all day and set up camp at night, sitting round the fire barbecuing steak and drinking shots of Jägermeister that Jacques kept in a freezer in the back of his car.

One night we heard something banging about among our pots and pans. Jacques unzipped the tent, saw a hyena a few feet away, rapidly zipped it back up and told us what was going on. I was so glad we all slept in one big tent – on my own I'd have been terrified. As it was I was still pretty nervous. Hyenas are large, carnivorous and have incredibly powerful jaws that could chew your arm off without much trouble.

'I'm going to stay here in the middle of the tent away from the sides, OK?' I said nervously, looking at Jacques who was reaching for the zip again. 'Maybe you should come away from the door.'

Jacques laughed. 'Don't be a wimp. It's not going to get in the tent. I'll scare it off.'

'What?! No, don't ...' but it was too late. Jacques had stuck his head out of the tent and was shouting and waving at the hyena, which after turning to snarl at him, ran off across the campsite.

'You're crazy!'

'That hyena knew it couldn't take me on,' he said with a wink. I shook my head and went back to bed. Jacques really was a man of the bush and completely fearless.

After the camping trip I stayed in Jacques' staff house back at the game reserve. He went back to working with volunteers and I got a voluntary job with a local company breeding horses and running horse trails. I helped with breaking in some of the sturdy young Arab horses and led groups of tourists on trails along the stunning sand dunes and wide, sandy beaches of the Eastern Cape.

One afternoon I was asked to ride one of the newer horses, a stallion, to help one of the trail leaders take a group of people out. The horse I was on kept acting strangely, shaking its head and hesitating. As we went to descend a large sand dune the horse lost its footing and fell, trapping my leg under it. We slid down the sandy bank until we hit a tree, at which point my left leg was trapped between the horse and the tree. I tried to get the horse to move, but it was unresponsive. I had to wait until the group leader, Jono, came back to find me and got the horse to its feet, freeing my leg.

By the next day my leg was black and I couldn't feel much below my knee. I saw a doctor, but there wasn't a lot to be done. I had severe soft-tissue bruising and nerve damage, and it would take time to recover. I would just have to wait and see if the sensation in my leg returned.

After a few days the bruising was healing and some of the feeling had returned, though my leg never completely recovered. Bored with being stuck in the house, I went back to work, where I discovered that the horse I had been riding was going blind. No one had realised until our accident.

A couple of weeks later I began to feel feverish and nauseous, and I ached all over. Another trip to the doctor confirmed that I had tick bite fever, caused by a bite from the tiny pepper tick. They're so small that you don't even realise you have one on you. The bite looks like a mosquito bite, and that's what I thought the innocent-looking mark on my hip was, until after a few days it had developed a brownish-black ulcerated scab that looked anything but innocent.

I felt so ill I thought I was dying but Jacques was relaxed about it. He'd had it several times and he knew the drill – antibiotics, lots of rest, fluids and time do the trick. He looked after me and reassured me that the first time you get it is the worst.

I looked at him in horror. I couldn't imagine having to go through it all over again.

I stayed for two months, working, lazing in the sun and spending time with Jacques. He was an Afrikaner and Afrikaans was his first language, though he spoke perfect English. He was into hiking and camping, cricket and rugby, and he cooked up a mean braai (Afrikaans for barbecue). But he was also thoughtful, concerned about animals and conservation, and bright; he was about to start a Masters degree in Environmental Management. Like me, he loved books, but while I enjoyed a good novel, Jacques preferred to spend hours poring over books on geology, the environment and wildlife. He had a thirst for knowledge and a passion for animals, and I really liked that about him.

I knew I couldn't possibly get involved with someone so far from home, especially not when I was just about to go to vet college and start a whole new phase of my life. So we became great friends and spent our evenings talking under the stars. Romance didn't happen until a year later, when I went back to do a work placement with Jono's horse trails company at the end of my first year of college. We were expected to get in some work experience every summer, so it was the perfect excuse to head back to South Africa.

Jacques invited me to stay with him again and one weekend, when he took the gap-year volunteers camping, I went along. We camped by a river and swam under the full moon. It was wonderfully romantic until Jacques insisted I stopped being a wimp about cold water, and picked me up and threw me into the deeper water. As I came up from under the water I glared at him, but he was just laughing, and I couldn't help laughing, too.

The next evening we all gathered for drinks in a tree-house that hung suspended in a huge tree in between Jacques' house and the house where the volunteers stayed. As everyone drifted off to bed Jacques and I were the only two left listening to the sound of the cicadas and the distant grunts of a lion. And that's when we looked at one another and realised that, no matter what the obstacles might be, we were kidding ourselves thinking that nothing could ever happen over long distance. We were perfect for each other and crazy about each other.

Four years on we were still together. In fact, I couldn't imagine wanting to be with anyone else. Jacques was studying for his Masters alongside work, he'd got the university job and I was on the last leg of my training. Between us we had criss-crossed the world many times, visiting one another, meeting each other's families and getting to know our very different cultures.

As soon as I got back home after each visit I started saving for my next air ticket and planning my next trip. But inevitably it could only be a handful of times a year and there were key moments in each other's lives that we missed.

This time I was combining my visit to Jacques for a short holiday with a work placement. College always encouraged us to get experience abroad and they were very happy to let me do some of my extra-mural weeks in South Africa.

I had been taken on by Thys, an old Afrikaner vet, deeply tanned with a white beard and an accent so strong I couldn't always understand him. I had first contacted him the previous year, when I'd emailed several vets working in the area where Jacques lived, but only Thys replied, warmly inviting me to go and work with him. That summer I flew out to see Jacques and met up with Thys, who immediately took me under his wing and treated me like a daughter. He called me Jo the Englishman, and when we were out working he'd call me Englishman and so would his clients. He was a real family man and he included me in his family with his wife, Johma, and son, Johannes, taking me back to their home for cold drinks and snacks in the breaks in between jobs. Thys lived on a large farm in the middle of nowhere, and despite the long days on the road he loved to come home in the evenings to help out on the farm. Johannes ran it while he was away, looking after the cattle they were rearing for market and the horses they bred for people who wanted to compete in endurance events.

As well as the cattle and horses, Thys had some rather interesting pets, which he took great delight in showing me. He had a whole pack of pitbull terriers, which he would let out at night to guard the house. I was a little nervous of pitbulls, given that they were illegal in England and all I had ever heard were horror stories about them, but Thys's dogs were far from savage. They were bouncy and playful, and true testament to the fact that dogs respond primarily to the way they are raised and treated.

But the pitbulls were definitely not the most unusual of Thys's pets. In a large pen behind his house he had a caracal, a species of wild cat with long ears. He had rescued it as a kitten after a farmer had killed its mother when she was hunting his sheep. Thys had raised it and now it stood about the size of a medium dog, but because it was tame he couldn't release it back into the wild. In addition to the caracal, Thys kept four crocodiles in a fenced area on his farm. He took great pride in his crocs, which were all fully grown and incredibly large.

'Come meet them,' he said to me one day.

'Erm, really? Are they not dangerous?' I enquired nervously.

'Yes. But it's a cold day. They will be slow, and you look fast,' he joked, and walked through the gate. I hesitantly came in after him. 'Watch where you're going, Englishman! I can only see three of them. I don't know where the last one is.'

I followed him, always making sure I had a clear path to the exit should something go wrong, but Thys was far from worried. He loved a bit of danger and thrived on the adrenaline.

'Look, you can touch it,' he exclaimed, demonstrating. The crocodile didn't stir. 'Go on!'

'Wow, um, OK.' I reached down to touch the bumpy skin at the base of the crocodile's tail, constantly keeping an eye on his head, which thankfully didn't move.

I turned to Thys. 'This is really surreal and fascinating, but equally terrifying. Can we please go now?'

'All right, Englishman.' With a last pat he turned from the croc and we headed for the gate.

Thys was always full of surprises. He spent his life in turquoise overalls, white wellington boots and a safari hat. He saw the occasional dog and did some wildlife work, but the bulk of what he did was looking after cattle on local farms. We would rattle up the red dirt roads in his old truck while Thys talked philosophy and I tried to ask him about his practice. He'd give me a brief answer and then go back to discussing existential theories and ideas about the origins of the universe, which all fascinated him.

The farms we visited were much more basic than British farms, and there was a far greater variety in size. The average farm in the UK has between 150 and 300 cows; in South Africa they either just have a few animals or upward of 1,000.

When we arrived at each remote farmstead, Thys got me involved in everything he did and was confident about throwing me in at the deep end. We'd herd the cows from the field into a smaller yard and then shoo them down the race. (A cattle race is also known as a chute, a run or an alley, depending on which country you're in. Both the UK and South Africa use the term 'race' for the narrow corridor built of parallel wooden fences into which cattle are herded, single file, so that we can line them up for examination.)

Thys and I would then go along the line of cows, checking them rectally for pregnancy, taking blood to look for any indicators of foot and mouth disease, or injecting the antigen for TB into their necks.

The problem was that these cows were wild Brahman beef cows, notorious for being jumpy and unpredictable, if not plain crazy. Brahmans have a hump and a dewlap –

a big flap of skin beneath the neck – and they're so highly strung that, unlike well-behaved (well, mostly) British cows, they regularly tried to jump out of the race and a couple always ended up hanging on the fence, front legs over and back legs still inside.

It was Thys who taught me the best way to do a pregnancy check on a cow. He insisted I go in with my left hand as the stomach is on the left-hand side of the cow, so the uterus is always pushed to the right. That makes it much easier to examine the uterus, instead of trying to contort the right arm backwards into an uncomfortable position.

It felt odd using my left hand at first, as I'm right-handed, but it was much easier to press down on the rim of the pelvis to feel for the uterus and see whether it was enlarged.

Thys was keen to give me experience, so when I mentioned to him that I hadn't done much work with pigs and didn't feel very confident with them he said, 'OK, Englishman, leave it with me.' A couple of days later, he said, 'There's a small rural community near here and I owe them a favour, so I offered to repay it by having you come and castrate their two boars.'

'Their what?'

'Boars. Don't worry, they'll be fine.'

When we arrived on the smallholding Thys turned to me. 'The owners have got no money for anaesthetic so the way we're going to do this is the old-fashioned way. We will inject the boars' testicles with barbiturates, and that will send them off to sleep as it is absorbed into the blood. But barbiturates are pretty dangerous drugs, so time is of the essence to castrate them before too much is absorbed.'

I looked at him in disbelief. Barbiturates are used to put animals down, and using minute amounts as an anaesthetic is old school and very dangerous. Use too much and they're dead. On the other hand, it's a whole lot cheaper than using modern anaesthetics. I made a mental note that I would never do this when I was qualified, but at that moment Thys was in charge.

'We'll get them up on the tailgate of my truck and you'll need to cut off the testicles while they're asleep. Just try not to be too slow about it,' Thys said, peering at me from under the rim of his safari hat.

'Thys, I'm not sure I can do this,' I said, looking anxiously at the emasculators he was laying out.

'Of course you can. And you'd better be quick about it,' he chuckled.

'I'd much rather you helped me, Thys.'

'Ah, you'll be fine, Englishman.'

And with that he rounded up the two boars, injected them, and once the first was asleep he heaved it onto the tailgate of his truck. Then he picked up his video camera, stood back and started filming.

I took a deep breath, I'd done this on a horse but never before on a pig. I looked at the boar's extremely large testicles. They were as big as grapefruit. I was going to have to cut the skin on the scrotum, push out the testicles, then apply the emasculators, which both cut off the testicle and clamped the blood vessels of the stump left behind. The clamp has to be the side of the animal, the cutter the side of the testicle. I remembered being told 'nut to nut'. There was a nut and bolt on the emasculator, and the side of the nut had to be the side of the testicle, to make sure they were the right way around.

'Come on, Englishman,' Thys roared. 'You've got about two minutes before you really need to be done.'

I grabbed the blade in one hand, the scrotum of the boar in the other – and cut through the skin.

Two minutes later the boar was stirring and his testicles lay on the ground at my feet. Our method may not have been clinical, conventional or elegant, but it did the job and Thys, roaring with laughter, slapped me on the back. 'Well done, Englishman, well done!'

After my fortnight with Thys, I had two weeks' holiday to spend with Jacques before my flight home. We went on a lot of game drives, often taking a picnic with us and spending the whole day in the reserve. As we drove, Jacques told me tales of animals in the wild, their environment and the delicate ecosystem that they depend on for survival. His eyes were like those of a hawk. He would see a small speck on the horizon and be able to tell it was a rhino, or a black dot far above in the air and identify what sort of bird it was. Until then I had thought my eyes were pretty good but I made a mental note to get them checked.

At one of our picnic stops I laid out a delicious ciabatta loaf I'd bought that morning. I turned to call Jacques and looked back to find a cheeky little vervet monkey clutching my bread. 'Oi, give that back,' I shouted, grabbing the other end of the loaf. For a second we both pulled, until the monkey bared his extremely sharp little teeth. I hesitated, and that was it. With one deft yank, he pulled the loaf out of my hand and headed up the nearest tree, where he sat munching on it while I glowered at him. Jacques thought it was hilarious – until he realised there was no bread for lunch.

When we weren't out looking at game we headed for the beach. One spot in particular was our favourite. On a beautiful large sand dune, covered in small bushes and flowers, there was a sandy clearing, and from it an incredible view across the ocean and further along the beach. We would sit there looking out to sea, regularly spotting whales, or pods of dolphins playing in front of us. It was the spot where I hoped Jacques might propose to me one day – I'd certainly dropped enough hints! We knew that we wanted to be together but, as Jacques pointed out, we had a few things to sort out first, like which side of the world we would live on. We both had work, families and lives in our different continents. Bringing them together permanently would mean making a lot of tough decisions.

When the time came to leave at the end of my stay, I didn't want to go. The thought of leaving Jacques for several months was miserable. I had kissed Jacques goodbye and was heading for the departure gate, in floods of tears, when I bumped into Thys, who was flying up to Johannesburg for a veterinary conference for a few days.

He patted my shoulder. 'Don't cry, Englishman,' he said. 'We'll see you again soon.'

CHAPTER FIVE

'What Seems to Be the Problem?'

'So, Jo, what do you think is wrong with its toes?'

I peered at the little creature in front of me.

'Er, they seem to be necrotic?'

'Yes.' Nadene was standing on the other side of the table, looking at me expectantly.

'And why would its toes be in this state?'

I kept peering, as though the answer might suddenly leap out at me. Why would a little leopard gecko, no more than eight inches long, have blackened toes that appeared to be dying?

It was a striking little creature – yellowish skin with black spots (hence the leopard part), L-shaped legs sticking out at right angles, its toes splayed out like little hands. Three toes on one of its front feet were blackened, and a toe on the other front foot was missing. It was staring at me as if it, too, were waiting for an answer.

Then I noticed little bits of dried skin on its feet. My

brother Ross had once had a leopard gecko, and I remembered how we would watch it in fascination as it shed its skin like a worn-out stocking, eating it as it peeled away.

'It looks as though it hasn't completely shed its skin. Could the remnant left behind be causing the blood flow to restrict in the toes?'

Nadene smiled. 'I think you're right. It's not an easy one, this, but that looks like the most obvious answer. Let's tell the owner to get baby oil and cotton buds and try to get those last remnants of skin off. That should at least save the remaining toes.'

I was in my first week at the Beaumont Sainsbury Animal Hospital, a clinic run by the Royal Veterinary College and situated next door to their Camden campus. Beaumont was a first-opinion practice for small animals, but it also had the only specialist exotics centre in central London – hence the steady stream of reptiles, birds, fish, and invertebrates such as snails and worms arriving though its doors. It's amazing what people decide to keep as pets.

Along with the others in my rotation group I was at Beaumont to practise consultations, straightforward treatments like vaccinations and puppy advice, basic surgery like neutering and dental care, and a little bit of exotics work alongside Nadene, an expert in her field.

Beaumont is a busy clinic based in a large four-storey building. It offers discounted rates to pet owners because there are a lot of vet students and trainee veterinary nurses working there. A constant stream of people and pets comes through the door. Since returning from South Africa my feet hadn't touched the ground and, as much as I missed Jacques, I'd barely had time to talk to him.

We worked early or late shifts, starting at eight or eleven in the morning. All the arrivals at Beaumont were logged on to the computer and we would each take the next case on the list as we became free. After going through a thorough history of the animal with its owner, asking all about the problem and doing a physical examination, we had to report back to the clinician in charge with our findings and recommendations. They would then return with us to see the patient, plus owner, and either opt for tests or prescribe medication.

These were our first full solo consultations without supervision and the vets in charge expected us to be very thorough indeed. We couldn't just ask, 'When was your dog last treated for fleas?' We had to ask what product was used and how often. This could mean quite lengthy consultations, as we worked our way through a seemingly endless list of questions, but it did teach us good practice and ensure that we didn't miss any vital information.

I enjoyed consultations because I never knew what, or who, was coming through the door. I loved chatting to the clients, and enjoyed meeting the variety of people and animals that arrived. As long as I started with 'What seems to be the problem?' the rest would flow and I felt my confidence growing with every case.

'Mr Grey with Ruby?' I announced, looking around the crowded waiting room.

'Here, over here.' Mr Grey, looking very flustered, shot out of his seat and hastened towards me, dragging a reluctant greyhound behind him.

'Oh, I am relieved to see you. I've been so worried about poor Ruby, she's in a terrible state,' he gasped. 'She's our angel, you know. We just dote on her and we can't bear to see her suffer. She gets the best of everything, so I just can't imagine what's gone wrong. And the worst part is that poor Ruby is so embarrassed about it.'

As I ushered him through to a consulting room, aware that the remaining owners in the waiting room were transfixed, Mr Grey talked non-stop and with such speed that it was hard to keep up. Waving his arms in the air and gesticulating theatrically, he threw himself into the chair and bemoaned poor Ruby's condition and her mortification.

Ruby, meanwhile, settled patiently beside him looking, if anything, mildly bored. She probably just felt rather unwell.

'So I see from the notes that she's got diarrhoea?' I ventured.

'Yes. Oh, my goodness, how could she have got it? We give her organic food; no rubbish at all for our Ruby.'

I tried to reassure him. 'Please don't worry too much. It's not uncommon, even in dogs that are very well cared for.'

I had flicked through Ruby's history before calling them in and it seemed that she had always been a perfectly healthy dog. The likelihood was that the diarrhoea was simply a reaction to something she'd eaten or perhaps a mild stomach bug.

I went through a detailed history, which Mr Grey was only too happy to supply, starting with the moment he and his partner first set eyes on little Ruby when she was just eight weeks old. 'It was love, you see.' His eyes grew moist. 'We loved her, and she loved us. We promised right then that we would always be there for her.'

'And you certainly are,' I said brightly. 'Now, let's get Ruby to stand up and I'll examine her.' I did, very gently and very thoroughly. She was a little bit dehydrated (cue another outburst from Mr Grey along the lines of, 'Oh, my poor Ruby') but otherwise there was not much to find.

Leaving Mr Grey and Ruby in the consulting room, I went back to relay everything to Harry, the vet in charge. He came back with me and we prescribed a diet of chicken and rice, as well as some binding paste.

'She will get the very best chicken that we can find, fresh every day, and I will cook it for her with the finest basmati rice,' Mr Grey informed us solemnly.

Thanking us profusely he headed out again towards the

waiting room with the reluctant Ruby in tow. He got to the end of the corridor and struggled with the door. Whoever designed the place put a release button on the wall to open the door and, goodness knows why, decided to place it several metres away so that, without fail, every client ended up tugging on the locked door for a while before realising that there was something they had to press to get out. 'Button on the wall,' I called, and a relieved Mr Grey finally made a rather agitated exit.

A few days later Ruby reappeared on my list of consults. My heart always dropped a little when an animal was brought back because it usually meant that the advice we had given hadn't worked.

'Oh, I'm glad it's you again,' Mr Grey began, as he sprang to his feet in the waiting room. 'Ruby likes you, so we were hoping it would be you. She didn't want to have to get to know someone else.'

Flattered as I was, I doubted that Ruby had even registered me, let alone taken a liking to me.

This time Mr Grey and Ruby went away with some antibiotics and a few days later he popped back to tell me that all was well – Ruby and her doting owners were restored to harmony. 'I'm so glad,' I told him, and I was. There's nothing like a satisfied customer, and Mr Grey and Ruby – he being so extravagant in all he said and did, and she so placid and patient – had made me smile.

That morning, in a rare moment off I caught up with Lucy over a coffee. 'How's the dating going?' I asked her. 'Found anyone you like yet?'

Lucy made a face. 'I haven't had a lot of time lately. I'm having real trouble with my research project. All my tests are failing and I'm beginning to panic, so the hunt for Prince Charming has had to go on the back burner, although I did have a quick flick through some dating profiles the other day. Just have a look how gorgeous this guy is,' she said, getting out her phone to show me the picture.

'He's nice,' I agreed. 'Why not go on a date?'

'I told you, no time. I'll save him for later and hope he's still free.'

In addition to all our placements, we each had to carry out and write up a piece of original research. Mine was on horses' shoes and whether horses are actually better off with or without them, and Lucy's was on cow's milk. She was trying to find out whether you could test the DNA in a particular cow's milk to see whether the cow would genetically have the potential to have a high milk yield. If it worked it would mean that in the future farmers would be able to test a cow's milk in her first lactation to see if she was going to be a high producer later in life. A great idea, as it could change the way that farmers select their cows for breeding. Apart from the small problem that Lucy wasn't getting any usable results.

I sympathised. It wasn't easy fitting in the research and I was getting a bit worried about my own, which was going to involve photographing an awful lot of horses. But we had a research month coming up, mid-May to mid-June, when we'd be able to catch up with the practical side and start putting it all together. Comforting ourselves with that thought, we headed back to work.

That afternoon I was due in surgery and I couldn't wait. I'd watched plenty of operations, and I'd scrubbed in and assisted at quite a few, but now I was going to be doing the whole thing on my own and I was really looking forward to it. There was something about surgery that I found deeply satisfying. I like working with my hands and I enjoy a bit of neat stitching, but the real buzz came from being able to make a real difference, right there and then.

My first solo op was a bitch spay on a young Staffie called Melissa. The supervising clinician was a very serious young vet who expected me to know exactly what I was doing and to talk him through every step of the procedure as I went along, which wasn't easy. He added comments and instructions at the same time, along the lines of 'Don't pull so hard, take that across, you need to ease off now.' It was all constructive criticism, but he was so deadpan that by the time I got to the end I wasn't sure whether he thought I'd done a good job or couldn't wait to see the back of me.

Luckily he seemed to think I was all right. When it was all over he smiled, for the first time, and said, 'You're a natural, well done.' I thanked him and walked out – and then did a little jig in the corridor. It was fantastic to have praise, especially from someone who I could see didn't give it lightly.

Over the next few days I removed an abscess from a rabbit, spayed a cat and castrated a tiny Chihuahua cross-breed. When it arrived in the surgery I took one look at this minute dog and wondered if I'd even be able to find its testicles. On most dogs they're about the size of plums, but this little chap's were more like peas; they were the tiniest testicles I'd ever seen, which made removing them very fiddly indeed. I kept finding them and then losing them again, and with the clock ticking and the clinician watching it was a bit nerve-wracking.

But by the end of the first week I was beginning to feel like a real vet.

Heady with triumph, on the Friday of my first week I met up with my old friend Abi for dinner. Abi and I had known one another since we met at the stables when she was eleven and I was thirteen. She was as mad about horses as I was, and we used to ride together every evening and at the weekends. When we got a bit older we had girly movie nights and went out to Saturday night parties together. We looked alike, so everyone took us for sisters, which I loved because I don't have a sister of my own.

Abi is a kind and gentle person, and I've never heard her say a bad word about anyone. After finishing her history degree she decided to train as a teacher with Teach First, the scheme that selects people who haven't trained as teachers, trains them for six weeks and then puts them into tough schools in low-income communities for the next two years. If they make it through that, they become qualified teachers. It's a great scheme, aimed at ending inequality in education and finding inspirational people to help and encourage kids who might otherwise fail, but the reality for Abi was pretty harsh. She was in a school where her Year 3 seven- and eight-year-olds gave her constant grief, and because Abi just wasn't the kind of person who would ever shout at them if they misbehaved they took ruthless advantage of her. The last time I'd seen her she had been pretty miserable.

'I'm ravenous,' I said as we pored over the menus in a little Italian bistro round the corner from Beaumont. 'I could eat everything here, and be back for more.'

Abi laughed. 'Anyone would think you're still growing, Jo, with the amount you seem able to put away.'

'It's being a vet, Abi,' I said. 'All that stress and tension just makes you want to eat. And speaking of stress and tension, how are things in the classroom?'

'Better.' She grinned. 'I've got a fantastic new trick. I have a timer and every time the children play up I run it for a minute. At the end of the lesson, the minutes on the timer come off their break. They only have to see me reach for the timer and they start yelling, "No, Miss, don't do that!" They're little angels now.'

'That's fantastic. Any chance you could come up with something to keep unruly pets and their owners in line?'

We spent the rest of the evening eating and talking non-stop. At 10.30pm I looked at my watch. 'Abs, I'm going to have to run. My last train goes in fifteen minutes.'

As she headed back to Kent for a weekend of catching up with her family, I made the forty-minute journey from Kings Cross to Welham Green. No visit home for me – weekends were Beaumont's busiest time and I had Saturday surgery the next day.

My second week at Beaumont was as full as the first. I did some more exotic animal work with Nadene. Among our patients were lizards, tortoises, a chinchilla (a South American rodent a bit bigger than a ground squirrel) and a Richardson's ground squirrel, which looked like a cross between a squirrel and a gerbil, and was the most manic little creature I'd ever seen. It went crazy, trying to scratch its way out of its box and then running all over the consulting room when we took it out. Keeping it still enough to clip its ingrowing nails was almost impossible.

The most exotic patient of all was an Asian water dragon, a gorgeous, bright green, lizard-like creature a couple of feet long. It had a bound egg, which meant that it had an egg inside it that it was unable to lay. After talking to the owner, a rather grumpy teenage boy, we suggested that he improve the dragon's habitat. Without the right environment they won't lay; she needed a nice wet corner with lots of damp moss for her to burrow down in to lay her eggs.

My time at Beaumont had been busy and fascinating, and I'd loved my stint there, but I was looking forward to a whole month at home in which I could work on my research project and catch up on some sleep.

The issue I'd chosen as my research subject – whether or not horses benefit from wearing shoes – had been causing a lot of controversy in the equine community. For hundreds of years horses have been shod, but a lot of people were beginning to wonder whether the shoes actually did any good, and increasing numbers of people in the horse world believed they actually damaged the hooves.

There were a lot of arguments on both sides, but no research had been published, so I hoped mine might be the first. We had to choose our research projects at the beginning of rotations, but when I went to see one of the equine clinicians at college to ask them to supervise me they said there would be far too much work involved, I would never manage to do it and I should pick another subject. A second one was also doubtful and I was beginning to wonder if I really had bitten off more than I could chew. I decided to give it one more try, and thankfully the third clinician, an equine orthopaedic specialist named Dave, liked the idea and agreed to be my supervisor. I enjoyed working with Dave; relaxed and always complimentary, he was an expert in his field and was always coming up with interesting points to consider.

The idea of the research was to photograph the hooves of horses with and without shoes, and to analyse the results. I needed to photograph a couple of hundred horses, but they couldn't be just any horses; they had to be in two distinct groups – horses that had worn shoes for more than eighteen months and horses that had not worn shoes for eighteen months, either because they'd had them removed or because they'd never been shod. It takes a year for a horse's hoof to grow out fully after a shoe is removed, which is why they would need to be unshod for a year and a half, to ensure the hoof had not been influenced by a shoe.

I would need to photograph each hoof from three angles and then analyse the results, taking measurements of the hooves from the photographs. My conclusions had to be written up as a 4,000-word piece of research, to be submitted to the college as part of my finals.

It was a big project, I knew that, but it was something in which I had a genuine interest. I made a list of places in the Kent area where I might find the horses I needed.

Then, in the first week of my research, I became ill. I had an agonising sore throat and a high fever. I felt awful. I went to the doctor three times and went through a whole lot of antibiotics before tests confirmed it was glandular fever.

There was no putting off the research – it had to be done because there was no other free time – so I was just going to have to toughen up. So every day, ignoring my raging temperature, I dragged myself out to local farriers, stables, vet practices and farms. I got through it by dosing myself up with paracetamol and sleeping whenever I wasn't work-ing. My parents were away on holiday for two weeks during that month, so I had Tosca and Paddy to look after as well as my horses.

It was a tough time and I felt pretty sorry for myself, regularly messaging Jacques to have a good moan. He was calm and patient, putting up with my self-pity and making me laugh despite my aches. By the end of the month I was really pleased with the work I'd done, though. I still had a long way to go before it would be completed, but the research so far was beginning to convince me that shoes really did alter the shape of a hoof, a conclusion I knew would put a few backs up but which really excited me.

Towards the end of my month at home I was finally starting to get better and had some more energy. At that point the social secretary of our year sent around an email asking if anyone would like to be involved in organising our graduation ball. Thinking it would be my last chance to have an impact on university life I jumped at the idea and agreed to be part of the committee. We decided to have a meeting straight away, and fifteen of us got together to start planning the biggest party of our lives. It had to be huge and it had to be memorable, as it was going to be the last time many of us would see each other before leaving to start our lives as vets, spread out across the country.

CHAPTER SIX

For the Love of Horses

She was beautiful. A young thoroughbred with a glossy black coat, huge dark eyes and a thick, dark mane. But with a huge bandage wrapped around her middle and a line running from a vein in her neck to four drip bags suspended above her, she looked a sorry sight.

I stepped into the stable beside her and stroked her neck. 'Hello, Ebony. You've had a tough time, haven't you?'

Her head was drooping towards the floor and she barely responded to my touch or my voice. She'd been through surgery the night before and now it would be a tense wait to see whether she would recover. Surgery on horses is complicated; a lot of owners won't even try it, preferring to put their horses quietly to sleep. But Ebony was young and strong, and she stood a good chance of pulling through.

It was my first day of equine medicine and I was in my element. I'm fond of all animals, but I have a connection with horses that goes back to when I was four years old and fell in love with them, so equine medicine was always going to be one of my favourite rotations. And thanks to my two, I'd already had a fair bit of experience with horse maladies and conditions. Elli and Tammy had been my world all through my teens and they were both seriously spoilt; they lived easy lives doing a bit of gentle work a few times a week but otherwise they spent their days as expensive lawnmowers in a field at the local stables. They both had thoroughbred in them, though, and despite all that pampering, over the years they'd been through just about every orthopaedic problem a horse could possibly have, and plenty of other health issues, too. Between them they'd had bone spavin (arthritis of the hocks), arthritis of the coffin joints, navicular syndrome, splints, collateral ligament injuries, tendon injuries, hoof abscesses and hoof wall defects. Thoroughbreds seem less hardy and more prone to general problems than other horse breeds, so I felt pretty well prepared for whatever equine medicine might throw at me.

For this rotation we were back in the RVC's state-of-the-art equine referral hospital. We'd already spent a week there for equine imaging at the start of rotations so we knew the layout of the place pretty well, but this time we would be working as members of the clinical teams, which was a lot more interesting.

It was also Grace's first day of filming for the *Young Vets* series. She wasn't at home around horses, and with a film crew following her every move and a camera peering over her shoulder the pressure was going to be on for her. She had warned the rest of us to get ready for potential background appearances and that set off alarm bells, because ours isn't a job that lends itself to glamour. Most days I leave the house with no make-up, my hair scraped back and dressed for encounters with mud, pet hair, drool and a variety of other noxious substances. But that morning, with my upcoming two seconds of fame in mind, I'd put on a bit of make-up, tied my hair into a French plait and put on my favourite pink and purple checked shirt. Not that anyone would see it, since we would be spending the day swathed in green overalls.

Feeling if not exactly showstopping then at least presentable, I arrived by the whiteboard in the barn at eight. Lucy, Katy and Jade were all there, and there was a definite whiff of anxiety in the air. The combination of horses and TV cameras was worrying them, too.

When Grace arrived, with a pile of equine textbooks under her arm, the film crew were following behind. Grace looked relieved to see us. She introduced us to Amy and Sam who we would get to know well over the next few weeks. Amy, short with blonde, curly hair, was the assistant producer. Smiling and bouncy, she was great at knocking away those camera nerves and making us laugh. Sam, the cameraman, was easygoing and friendly, and kept telling us he'd filmed for *Countryfile*, which I think he felt qualified him for anything to do with animals. However, we soon discovered that neither of them had much horse sense at all; they would go too close, make too much noise and hold a sound boom right over a horse without realising that horses are very easily spooked, especially by objects they've never encountered before. We had to give them a rapid but very brief insight into the horse world, along the lines of, 'Don't stand too near the horses, don't hold cameras and booms over them, under them or anywhere near their heads, and don't go round the back of them, especially sick horses, which are even more likely to kick out at you than well ones.'

The whiteboard in the barn was where all the current cases were listed, and once we were all there, Imogen, the clinician in charge, dished them out between the students. Ebony had come in the night before with colic and a displaced intestine, and had gone straight to surgery. Now she needed hourly checks and I leaped at the chance to look after her.

'Colic' is a broad term for abdominal pain. It's common in horses, and frequently we have no idea what has caused it. The animal may just have some spasms, or it might be very gassy, but it could be more serious, too, such as an impaction of food, or part of the intestine could have become displaced or entrapped. Colic can even be down to problems with the uterus or ovaries.

Some colic is simple and can be easily sorted with time and pain relief, but in other cases, when the gut has got twisted or entrapped, fluid, gas and food matter, known as ingesta, build up behind the obstruction and it's very serious. When Ebony arrived she had been showing clear signs of pain and distress, which indicated that this might be what was happening in her case. Horses in this state often sweat and look agitated – they kick at their abdomen with their back legs, turn to look at their flanks or lie down and roll repeatedly.

Ebony had been operated on to correct the displacement and remove the build-up of matter in her gut.

Whenever possible, if the clinical problem allows for it, vets like to do standing surgery, sedating the horses so that they're sleepy and then given a local anaesthetic on the operation site. Operations such as castrations, spinal surgery, head surgery, stitch ups and some orthopaedic surgeries can be done like this. But in cases like Ebony's, where a major operation is necessary, they have to be fully anaesthetised. For this they're taken into specially kitted-out knockdown surgical suites, in which the floor and walls are covered with thick padding. Once the anaesthetic is administered the horse will be out cold within seven heartbeats, which is around twenty seconds. After that, five or six people will snap into action; one will intubate the horse (put a tube down its windpipe to help it breathe), others will put shackles on its legs and attach it to a crane that will then lift the horse onto the operating table, which has raised sides so that the horse can't fall off it. Once there the shackles are removed and the horse is attached to the anaesthetic machine and carefully monitored during surgery.

Still woozy after the operation, Ebony was now in the Intensive Care Unit, a stable block that you can only enter when wearing fully sterile kit – even to step into her stable I had to go through boot dips and then put on a sterilized waterproof top, and gloves. Kitting up took a full five minutes before I went in to see her, then another five taking it all off again, and I needed to do that every hour.

Because this kind of surgery is very risky for horses it was a big thing for Ebony's owners to decide to try it. But the alternative would have been to lose her – she would have had to be put to sleep, and that would have been a real tragedy for a young horse with loads of potential. So despite the risk, and the cost, they had opted to give her a chance and I wanted to do everything possible to help make sure that she made it.

Days two to five after surgery are known as the 'danger zone', in which a horse has to be very carefully monitored.

A high percentage of horses relapse and either get colic again or the surgical site breaks down and becomes infected. If the intestine has been damaged by having the blood supply compromised then breakdown is far more likely.

During the first three days the horse has to be checked every hour. My checklist included looking at her gums to see that she wasn't anaemic and to check her blood pressure was still good, taking her temperature to check it hadn't spiked, which would indicate infection, listening to her heart-rate to make sure it wasn't speeding up (a possible sign of pain), listening to her guts to see if they were nice and noisy, which would mean they were working again, and checking the pulses in her fetlocks to make sure they were calm and not bounding. A bounding pulse can indicate laminitis, an inflammation of the lamellae (the bits that hold the hooves onto the legs), which is possible after surgery or when toxins have been released from a compromised gut, and it can rapidly become so serious that the horse has to be put down.

Determined to be thorough and not to miss anything, I was spending fifteen to twenty minutes working through these checks, and with the time involved in kitting up and then taking all the gear off again, it was taking half an hour out of every hour.

To add to the complications, Grace was coming with me some of the time to learn how to do colic checks, and of course Amy and Sam were following Grace. So there were four of us, plus the camera and sound mic, crowded into the stable and, conscious that I didn't want to get anything wrong when it was being recorded on film, I went through the colic checks even more slowly.

Any thoughts of glamour had gone out of the window early on, as taking the sterilized top on and off had made my hair look as though I'd just got out of bed, and I was wiping the sweat off my brow with my arm as I worked so I'd long since wiped off the make-up I'd carefully applied that morning.

Grace was worried about how to do colic checks and I was happy to show her where to place the stethoscope to listen to the guts most effectively and where to place your fingers to feel the digital pulses in the legs. I enjoyed showing her but, conscious of the cameras in front of us, I was distracted and stumbled over my words. I just hoped they wouldn't use that footage, as I was pretty sure I came across as a babbling mess.

Vets can't really afford to become too attached to any particular animal. We see so many that are sick and vulnerable, but in order to help them we have to take a step back emotionally and be the scientists that we are; analysing, observing and judging what will be best for them. But every now and again, despite our best efforts, an animal gets under our skin and we just can't help feeling a deeper connection. It was like that for me with Ebony; she was such a gallant horse and so very unwell that my heart went out to her.

Ebony tolerated my checks patiently, and as I went about them, taking care not to startle her, I spoke to her gently, soothing her and encouraging her to get well again.

'Come on, my lovely,' I whispered into her neck. 'You can do it.'

On the second day we needed to encourage her to eat very small amounts. But despite being offered hay and haylage, a softer, sweeter type of hay, she remained unresponsive. In the hope that it might appeal to her, I went out and picked some grass and brought it in for her. To my delight she nibbled at it.

I stroked her neck. 'So that's what you fancy, is it? Well, there's plenty more where that came from.'

As soon as she was allowed out I put a bridle on her and took her up to a lovely clearing close to a field where the university's own horses were. It was quiet and open there, and much nicer for her than grazing on a grass verge by the little roads that wound their way around the campus.

I began to gently groom her, running a big brush over her neck and shoulders, being careful to avoid the bandage around her middle. And before I finished work for the day and handed over to the night shift, I would go and pick buckets full of grass, so that they could feed them to her.

Ebony's owner came in to see her every couple of days. She lived several hours' away, so she couldn't make it more often than that, and she usually arrived with her two young children in tow. The whole family clearly loved Ebony. They'd bred her and they planned to use her for show jumping when she was a bit older, but right now they were enjoying having her as part of the family. They would pet and fuss over her and ask all kinds of questions about how she was. It was lovely to see how much they cared about her.

By day three she appeared to be doing well. She accepted some fresh haylage along with her grass and she began to look brighter. Her hourly colic checks were reduced to two-hourly. But on the fourth morning, when I arrived for work, I learned that overnight her temperature had spiked and as a result the surgeons and clinicians were very concerned. The colic checks were once again hourly, with someone doing LOBD checks – Look Over the Barn Door – every half an hour to see how she was doing.

A few hours into the day I went to check on her and found her lying down, looking miserable and grunting. And then she started to roll.

Afraid that she was seriously relapsing I rushed to see Imogen. She told me to go with the intern on duty, collect Ebony and bring her round to an examination room for a full work up while they rang the surgeons to have them on standby in case she needed to go back to surgery. We got Ebony gently to her feet and led her to one of the pristine examination rooms, where an ultrasound scan of her abdomen and a rectal examination revealed that her guts appeared to be healing well. Then her belly bandage was taken off, and we had our answer; Ebony's metre-long surgical wound had become sore and infected. While any complication wasn't ideal, it was a huge relief that she didn't need to go back for another operation. The mortality risk of horses in surgery is scarily high, and even more so the second time around.

She was already on the standard post-surgery horse antibiotics of penicillin and gentamicin, known as pen and gent, which were administered by injection. Now we added stronger antibiotics to fight the infection. A day later Ebony was picking up again, and once more we heaved a sigh of relief. She was a fighter.

The following day we had a new patient arrive, a very small rescue pony called Tinker. He was a friendly little chap, only twelve hands high, dark brown with a white streak down his nose and white socks. Tinker had been rescued by the RSPCA after being found in a pretty poor condition, badly underweight and neglected. Now he had a new family, young mum Molly and her two small children, and with his new family's love and kindness he was gradually being restored to good health.

Tinker had come in with a lump on his face that was clearly bothering him. Poor Molly was dreadfully worried, and it worried all of us, too. You can't see a lump on an animal without being concerned that it could be cancer. He needed a CT scan, but he was so small that he had to be propped up on wooden blocks so that he could reach his head into the scanner. To everyone's relief, a scan confirmed that the lump was a tooth abscess. Very painful for poor Tinker, but not life-threatening.

The operation to remove his infected tooth was one that could be done with him sedated but conscious. Tinker was Grace's case, so she was helping with the surgery while I stroked his neck to reassure him. It's not easy to extract a large horse tooth that is tightly wedged between two others, so loosening it with a clamp took over an hour. Thankfully, as Grace wriggled the large clamp back and forth, Tinker was so heavily sedated that he was barely aware of what was going on, and eventually his tooth was safely removed, fully intact. Tinker was brilliant throughout, and after the op he was led back to his stall to recover and given antibiotics to deal with the abscess. He made a full recovery and went home a couple of days later with a very happy and relieved Molly.

The following week I switched to the night shift. This meant arriving at six in the evening for rounds; the hand-over from the day staff. All staff on both shifts had to be present, which meant it had to be delayed until anyone still in surgery was finished. During rounds the day student in charge of each case would present it, giving us an update on the horse, its condition and any treatment or care it would need overnight.

Nights tended to be quieter; we had regular checks to do, but, apart from one or two emergencies, the five of us spent a fair bit of time watching movies, eating popcorn and playing with Grace's video diary. ITN Productions had given it to her to record the goings on of the night, as understandably they didn't want to sit with us from 6pm to 7am, waiting for something that might or might not happen. The idea was for Grace to record how she was feeling, and a bit of the action, but we ended up filming through a window, with one or two of us on the other side, pretending to go up and down stairs, or up and down an elevator. It was a lot of fun, until Grace handed back the camera a few days later and we realised that it could potentially appear in a BBC show that millions of viewers could watch.

Ebony was still with us in the stables and making steady progress. I went in to do her checks, which were now less frequent and to give her a nuzzle and have a chat. She was still being a picky eater, rejecting haylage that was more than a day old and preferring fresh grass, but that was fine, I was happy to nip out and pick a bucketful for her.

A couple of days into my night-shift week I learned that Ebony was going home the next morning. On the day, her owner arrived bright and early with the horsebox to collect her and we all came out to see them off. I gave Ebony a hug; I was truly happy that she had recovered – I knew that she would make a fine show jumper – but I was going to miss her.

On my next shift a little Falabella horse called Poppet arrived. Falabellas are the tiniest of all horses, perfect little creatures, sleek and compact, very like Shetland ponies but even smaller. Originally bred in Argentina, they're now found around the world. They're too small to be ridden, but they're popular as show horses and as pets.

Poppet was very unwell. Grey with white dapples, she was adorable to look at but was showing clear signs of distress and the clinician in charge was concerned. Like Ebony she had colic, but the hope was that we could clear it up without a major surgical intervention. She had an impaction, so she was put on a high rate of intravenous fluids to try to soften it and she was starved and given pain relief. We were told to give her an hourly colic check and to do a LOBD check every half hour in between. The problem was that Poppet was not much bigger than a largish dog and she couldn't get her head over the stable door to say hello to us.

We were stumped, until someone thought of opening the door and putting a bale of hay across it. Poppet could rest her chin on it, and we could check her more easily.

As the night wore on Poppet kept lying on her back and rolling from side to side. Because her colic was caused by a blockage in her gut that needed to shift, she was rolling to try to ease her discomfort and budge the impaction. But rolling repeatedly wasn't a good idea, as she could potentially cause herself further damage, so it was decided that one of us had to stay with her all the time, picking her back up and putting her on her feet every time she tried to lie down and roll.

In the early morning the decision was taken to tube her. Tubing is often the last stop before surgery. It involves putting a tube up the animal's nose and down into their stomach, sticking a funnel in the top and pouring in water. As the water goes down you pull out the funnel and direct the tube into a bucket underneath, to create a siphon that will suck out the liquid from the stomach. A horse's stomach normally contains an absolute maximum of two litres of fluid, although with a Falabella it would be half this. If there's significantly more than that it's a bad sign because it means there's a build-up. Horses can't vomit, so the excess matter just collects inside them and it can kill them.

Poppet responded well to this procedure, with her stomach contents cleared out she calmed down and stopped trying to roll, and by the next day she had passed some faeces – a sure sign that she was on the mend.

On my last morning, weary after a twelve-hour shift, I stood outside with Lucy, leaning on a fence, watching the sunrise.

'I've loved every minute of this placement,' I said. 'I'm going to miss being here when I'm on the farm next week.'

'Wish it was me,' Lucy sighed. 'I've got pathology for the next fortnight. I know I chose it, but now I can't think what came over me, I must have been mad. Looking down microscopes all day isn't going to be fun. It makes me dizzy, and half the time I have no idea what cells all the little dots are.'

'Could be worse, though,' I said, flicking a bit of dried manure off my boot. 'You could be in an abattoir. We've still got that to come next month.'

She made a face. 'You're right, that's not going to be a lot of fun. All right, I'll stop feeling sorry for myself. And in two weeks' time I've got work experience with a farm vet. Plenty of lovely cows to look forward to.'

We said goodbye to the staff, the other girls in our group and one another. For the next month we were all off to do separate electives and work experience.

Back at the house I poured myself a bowl of cereal and stroked Buddy, who was just getting out of his basket for a stretch. I opened the fridge to get some milk, and yelped. Sitting in the middle of the shelf was a cow's hoof. Which of my charming housemates had stuck that in there? I grabbed the milk and closed the fridge.

Minutes later John wandered into the kitchen in a T-shirt and pyjama bottoms, hair sticking out in all directions. 'Morning,' he said. 'How was the night shift?'

'Fine, how was pathology? And is that your cow's hoof in the fridge?'

'Oh, yeah, sorry. I thought it would be pretty cool to try to preserve it. We could put it on the shelf as an ornament when I've dried it out. I'll take it out later.'

'Sooner would be nice. And maybe give the inside of the fridge a wipe?'

He looked surprised. 'Really?'

'Mmm, I'm not sure cow's hooves are all that hygienic. Especially when they're tucked in between the butter and the eggs.'

'Oh, OK.' He wandered out again.

I reminded myself that I did choose to share a house with four boys, and there were many benefits, although most of them had temporarily slipped my mind.

I finished my cereal and headed off to bed.

CHAPTER SEVEN

Fly on the Wall

Two weeks in the Dorset sunshine seemed an inviting prospect. After a week of nights at the equine hospital it felt like an age since I'd seen daylight, so I was looking forward to being out in the fields working with farm animals.

Along with two other vet students, Alice and Danielle, I was staying in an adorable picture-postcard cottage in a pretty picture-postcard village with the distinctly unpicturesque name of Shittington – not that it bothered any of the local people, who were a lovely bunch.

The three of us were there to study farm animal population, which meant doing the rounds with the local farm vets. This was a little like the work we were doing in Wales, checking out the health of local herds, but this time we were allowed to do a lot more of the actual procedures; it was more hands-on and less to do with writing reports and adding up statistics, and my hope was that it would give my farm skills a real boost.

We spent the next two weeks taking blood from calves to assess how much immunity had passed on from the mother, and vaccinating calves and cows against BVD (Bovine Viral Diarrhoea) and IBR (Infectious Bovine Rhinotracheitis, a virus that affects the airways and fertility). Both are nasty viruses that can spread fast. As we'd already learned in Wales, the priority for farmers these days is to keep the herd healthy, so they're always on the watch for anything that might cause real problems.

In between vaccinations and taking blood samples I had fun learning how to use a pregnancy scanner and how to trim cows' hooves. The scanner is a sausage-shaped probe that you hold in your hand and insert into the cow rectally. It relays pictures back to a screen and gives a more detailed diagnosis of pregnancy than simply using your hand.

As for hoof-trimming, it's a bit like cutting your nails but a lot harder work! A cow's toes are covered by a thick coating of keratin, the same stuff our nails are made of, and like nails they keep growing. Cows need this trim one or twice a year, and the idea is to create a perfectly shaped hoof so that they can walk comfortably; we used hoof nippers and hoof knives to do this. I enjoyed shaping their hooves to make them nice and even, trimming off loose edges that could trap dirt, all the while checking for ulcers and spraying antibiotics if there were any signs of infections. The cows were, for the most part, very patient while we worked and I liked to think they appreciated the effort. The trimmings aren't just thrown away afterwards, they are kept and used to make the foam in fire extinguishers, among other things.

On the last day of the first week, while we were doing our thing down on the farm, I bumped into Isobel, the producer of *Young Vets*, who was scouting for filming locations for when Grace came to do her farm elective in a couple of months' time. She came to watch us at work, and we spent an hour or so chatting and explaining what we were attempting to do with the hooves of the cows. In return she told us a bit more about *Young Vets* and how it was all going. She explained that, contrary to what we all thought, it wasn't reality TV or a fly-on-the-wall programme, it was an observational documentary. Right, I thought, so there's a difference? Weren't they pretty much the same thing? I decided I'd better keep my thoughts to myself.

That night I dashed off to Kent for the weekend to go to Abi's birthday party. She'd just finished her first year as a teacher and she was in the mood to celebrate. We had a great night out and danced till one in the morning, so I arrived back in Dorset a little tired on Sunday evening.

After another week with the cows in the glorious Dorset countryside I headed back home to catch up with my family, before starting a fortnight's work experience with a sports horse veterinary practice that provided veterinary services for the local racecourse.

This was heady stuff; the idea of working with highly strung racehorses fascinated me. They are mostly hot-blooded thoroughbreds – tall, slim, athletic and handsome – but because of the exertion they are put under they have a high accident rate and a lot of health problems.

The first race I attended was on a Tuesday evening, which meant working a long day as I had started at eight that morning when we visited a number of local stables. I really didn't care, though, because I was so excited and couldn't wait to see behind the scenes.

We had been told to dress smartly, which was impractical but necessary according to the rules, so, in contrast to my usual dress-down, vet-on-the-go look, I wore smart beige tailored trousers with a crisp shirt, my freshly washed black Musto coat and polished boots.

Vets Jane and Tanya, both of whom, in their tailored outfits, looked more like race officials than vets, were warm and welcoming. Jane had just been made a partner of the practice, despite still being in her early thirties, and Tanya was a hugely experienced vet with loads of tips to pass on. They knew exactly what they were doing, oozed confidence and looked completely at home amongst the race officials and racegoers. I, on the other hand, felt totally out of place and would have been more at ease in my wellies mucking out the stable.

Just before the first race, the three of us went to stand in the middle of the parade ring amongst the trainers, owners and jockeys to assess how each horse was walking and to pick up any problems. Tanya and Jane were running me through a checklist of what to look out for when the first of the racehorses came through – and took my breath away. I had been around horses all my life, but I had never seen anything like these specimens. These were super-horses, the athletes of the horse world; every muscle popped from them, they were lean, their coats glistened in the low sunlight and their manes flowed. These were horses at their peak.

When the bell rang the jockeys mounted almost in unison. The horses seemed to know what the bell signalled and some of them started bouncing with excitement. The trainers led them down the walkway to the race track and, as the last one left the ring, we followed. Racegoers crowded towards the walkway on both sides, watching the horses and looking curiously at us. For a few heady moments I had a sense of what it must feel like to be a champion athlete, coming out of the tunnel onto the pitch, with a fever of excitement and expectation all around.

As the horses reached the racetrack, the trainers stepped back and the jockeys cantered them up to the start line.

That was our cue to head for the two BMW cars parked to one side. Tanya got into one to go to the halfway point, ready to cover the second half of the race, and Jane and I got in the other and headed for the start line. Once there we left the car to have a look at the horses waiting to go into the start gates, checking for a final time that none of them appeared lame or unwell. Some were playing up and refusing to walk in without a tussle but the jockeys knew how to manage them. As the last one was led into the stall, Jane and I sprinted back to the car.

We had just seconds before they released the horses. We dived into the car and accelerated to keep up with the horses. It was amazing being right next to the race with the horses galloping beside us, eyes wild and nostrils flaring. I was lost in awe of them, until Jane shouted 'Hold tight' and I bounced halfway out of my seat and hit my head hard on the roof. The smooth road beside the track had given way to a bumpy dirt track but we hadn't slowed down. We followed the horses for another couple of hundred metres until we reached Tanya's car. At that point she took over and followed the race back onto the smooth road on the other side of the track and on to the finish.

We followed more slowly, me rubbing my sore head as Jane apologised and explained that we absolutely had to keep up with the race. We reached the finish as the last horse was leaving the track, got out of the car and followed them back up the walkway to check that they were all being offered water and washed down, and that none had been hurt during the race. Jane was pulled aside by a trainer who wanted her to put a scope down one of the horses, as it hadn't run as well as they had expected. We took the horse back to the on-site vet room to put the camera down its windpipe. There was a little mucus, which indicated the start of a mild respiratory infection. This put the trainer's mind at rest; the horse wasn't useless, it was becoming ill.

Moments later we ran back to follow the horses into the next race. There were several races that night and we had a turnaround time of about ten minutes between each, so we didn't stop for several hours.

I loved my night at the races; the pace, buzz, the people, the excitement, and most of all those magnificent horses.

Two days later I received an email from the *Young Vets* programme makers to say that Isobel had loved meeting me and that she thought I would be great in the series. I was stunned; it took me a few moments to take it in. If I agreed, there would be a film crew following me through the rest of my rotations and I knew that would, at times, make life harder. But on the other hand it would be fun, and I would have a record of this year as a souvenir of one of the toughest and most challenging times in my life. How could I say no?

I wrote back to say I'd be delighted. The crew would join me, they said, in a couple of weeks' time, during my summer holiday with my family, to do some background filming.

After the heady thrills and glamour of working with sports horses and my invitation to be part of the *Young Vets* series I bumped back down to earth with a week in an abattoir in Bristol. This was not a placement that many of us trainee vets were looking forward to, but it was an essential part of our training. Every abattoir has a vet present to ensure that animals are treated humanely until the point of slaughter, and that the procedures are carried out properly and hygienically. The vet also provides a vital service to the meat inspectors who check the meat for any signs of disease before it goes on the market.

Determined to prove to myself that I had a strong stomach, I'd already visited an abattoir before I started at the RVC. It was not fun seeing a healthy cow and realising that half an hour later it would be dead, but I got through it and this time I was at least prepared for what would be involved.

So at the abattoir we were taught about animal welfare and meat inspection, and on the plus side I felt reassured that the meat we all eat is carefully monitored and the process is quick and pain-free for the animals, who are unaware of what's happening because they're stunned unconscious before slaughter.

It was good to be back with my rotation group after a month in which we'd all gone our separate ways to do our elective courses and our work experience. We worked in the abattoir from 6am to 1pm, so we had afternoons clear. There were a couple of assignments to write, but other than that we were free. As it was August and the students were on holiday, we were staying on the Bristol University campus, so Lucy and I headed for their impressive squash courts, figuring that if we could play tennis, squash couldn't be that hard.

Lucy was president of the RVC tennis team, regularly taking time off from rotations on Wednesday afternoons for matches, and while I wasn't as good as she was, I could play. But we soon discovered that when it came to squash our tennis skills meant nothing. We were so bad that we fell around laughing at ourselves.

At the end of the week I headed straight off on holiday, heady with the prospect of a whole week's holiday with my lovely family in Cornwall. Every year Mum, Dad, Ross and I go to the same little cottage in the Camel Valley Vineyard in north Cornwall and have a lazy fortnight pottering around beaches, walking the dogs, looking at holiday cottages and filling up with cream teas at Viv's cafe down the road.

This year I couldn't wait. The last few months had been non-stop, so a complete break from rotations, electives, work experience and the whole vet package was a wonderful prospect. But no, wait, hadn't I agreed that the TV crew could come and do some filming? Was I mad?

It was too late to back out, so I just had to hope that having the film crew around wouldn't mean too much disruption to our precious break.

In the end it was fine. The crew that came along were the two I knew well from our equine fortnight, Amy and Sam, and they didn't arrive until the Wednesday, so we had three whole days to ourselves first.

There's a dairy farm next to where we stay and over the years I had become friends with the owners. The current farmer, Tom, was eight years older than me and he'd taken over the running of the farm from his dad several years earlier. I did some work experience with them when I was sixteen and I'd been dropping by every summer since, so Tom and I had become good friends and he'd agreed that the crew could do some filming on the farm.

Tom is a country man through and through. All he ever wanted was to take over the family farm and to keep things just as they had always been. He loved the quiet life, running the farm and then going to the pub for a pint in the evenings. With my thirst for adventure we were very different, but he was a joker who made me laugh and I liked lending a hand when I was down there.

This summer Tom proudly showed me the trailer he had bought to fit behind the tractor. The idea was that it would pick up the cut grass and save him doing it by hand. Except that what Tom showed me was, as far as I could see, a pile of rusty junk.

'What do you think?' he said, eyes gleaming with triumph.

'Um, it looks as though it might need a bit of work doing on it.'

'Yes, I know, but never mind that, I'll soon sort it out. And it was a bargain at £800.'

I peered at the trailer, with its rusting sides, dodgy wooden flooring and rotting chains.

'I'm sure it will be great when you get it going, Tom.'

'Course it will. Real beauty this, it's going to save me hours of work.'

To be fair, he did get it going. He worked on it for a week and eventually it cranked into action and rattled along behind the tractor, flicking at least some of the grass into the back before grinding to a halt. A thump and a kick and it would reluctantly be off again, until the next stop, but despite its lacklustre performance and dubious charms, Tom remained delighted with it and was convinced that it was a bargain.

When Amy and Sam arrived on the farm they decided to shoot a dreamy (and I thought cheesy, but I kept quiet) segment of me walking through a herd of cows and then sitting down on the grass to admire the view. Unfortunately, however, I hadn't slept much the night before, and each time the camera panned around for a close-up shot of my face, my eye twitched convulsively, making me look more Hunchback of Notre-Dame than dewy-eyed young vet.

Giving up on that footage, they waited until the next day and joined us in the farmyard, where I was helping Tom 'dry off' some cows in the dairy parlour, which meant putting teat sealants in those cows that needed a few milk-free months before giving birth to another calf and starting the cycle again. As the camera panned in I concentrated hard on the teats of the cow I was under, trying to do a perfect job, but unfortunately I didn't think about where my head was and I head-butted the cow on the hock so hard that my head was left throbbing. Despite the pain I tried to ignore what had just happened and carry on but, unbeknown to me, I had cow dung smeared across my forehead, which didn't exactly make for a flattering bit of footage.

Third time lucky, we all hoped. The following day Amy decided they would film me with Tosca on the beach. What could be simpler than a little sequence of me playing with the family dog? Tosca, despite being blind, still had a springer spaniel attitude. In other words, she was a big ball of non-stop energy. I really hoped she would be reasonably calm and play her part, but with the scent of the sea in her nostrils she became wildly excited, tugging and jerking on her lead so that it twisted round my hand and I yelped in pain. 'Try squatting down beside her and giving her a cuddle,' suggested Amy.

I tried, pleading with Tosca to behave and just sit patiently for two minutes while we both stared out to sea. But Tosca wasn't having it; she bounded off into the waves, blissfully happy and oblivious to her missed opportunity to be a canine star.

Amy decided to cut straight to the family film. Mum wasn't keen on being filmed, so they went for a shot of me with Dad and Ross on either side. So far so good, and they asked Dad and Ross each to say something about me. Dad was very complimentary, but in true little brother style Ross wasn't. He and I just couldn't stop laughing, so yet another unusable piece of film bit the dust. All in all not a good start to my TV career!

I spent a final evening with Tom, enjoying a bottle of wine beside a fire in his backyard, talking about life and laughing about the filming. Despite our different takes on life I really liked Tom and I was sad to say goodbye for another year.

After we drove back from Cornwall I had one more relaxed Sunday before starting two weeks in anaesthesia, a rotation I was absolutely dreading. I did a bit of last-minute cramming, the names of all the different anaesthetic drugs blurring before my eyes and my panic levels rising, before giving up and nipping over to Grandma and Grandpa next door for a calming cup of tea.

Mum's parents have always been a mainstay in my life. They've lived next door to us all our lives, and when Ross and I were little and our parents were working they picked us up from school and fed us wickedly delicious food like chicken nuggets and Grandpa's amazing creamy mash or, our favourite of all, custard with chocolate drops sprinkled over it. We had some lovely times; Grandpa used to take me to the park to find a goose feather, bring it home and cut it into shape and then use it as a quill to teach me calligraphy. And Grandma taught me how to make melt-in-your-mouth scones and crunchy gingerbread men.

As I hugged them goodbye and piled my bags back into the car I thanked my lucky stars for my generous, supportive family.

CHAPTER EIGHT

We Saved a Life

We'd been told that the anaesthesia rotation would make even the toughest vet student cry. Rumour had it that the clinicians were merciless, the drugs impossible to figure out and the operations interminable. So I arrived at the Queen Mother Hospital at eight o'clock on a morning in late August feeling extremely nervous. I felt sure that I knew absolutely nothing and was going to fall flat on my face.

To make matters worse, the TV crew were coming to film me at work for the first time. After the slapstick carry-on of our holiday shoots, I could only hope that this wouldn't be a disaster, too.

Thankfully, two of the other students were also being filmed. Grace was by now a bit of an old hand in front of the cameras, and so was Charlie. He was in our sister rotation group, the one that was doing more or less the same order of rotations and had been with us in Wales. They joined us again for anaesthesia and it was good to see them

– especially Charlie, who was one of those guys that everyone got on with. Quite a posh country chap, he wore his checked shirts, chinos and gilet as standard wear rather than just as vet 'uniform'. With blond, floppy hair and a huge grin on his face, Charlie was always in a good mood, always jokey and easygoing, no matter how stressful the moment. And he was brave; he would give anything a go, even if he knew he was probably going to get it wrong.

I enjoyed bumping into Charlie in the student tea room, where we'd regularly congregate to have a moan. He'd be the one who would come and put his arms around you and say, 'How's it going? What's going on?'

That first week the crew concentrated on Charlie and Grace, and I was grateful for the chance to find my feet with anaesthesia without cameras there to highlight my every mistake. I like to get things right, which I was quickly coming to realise was unrealistic in rotations. This was the time to get things wrong and learn from those mistakes so that they wouldn't be made once we were out in the world on our own.

My first case was a sleek black cat called Archie, who had a mass in one of his lungs. He needed to have a third of the lung removed, which required a sternotomy, for which the whole sternum would need to be opened. When you do this the animal can't breathe alone, so it has to be attached to a ventilator that will effectively breathe for it. But ventilating has a major impact on blood pressure; if you over-ventilate it affects the blood flowing around the thorax and around the heart, and because of this you must take the blood pressure every five minutes. This is in addition to the information on the anaesthetic machine that must be closely monitored throughout the operation; the heart rate, oxygen saturation level (the amount of oxygen in the blood), the breathing rate, the end tidal CO_2 (which is the amount of carbon dioxide being breathed out), and finally the isoflurane concentration (which indicates the concentration of anaesthesia you are using).

As the operation is carried out you sit to one side with a chart in front of you, regularly noting the levels of all these different functions.

Adding blood pressure into the mix means putting a cuff around the animal's front leg, with a small probe positioned around the back of the paw. The probe is attached to a machine that lets you hear the pulse as a kind of puffing sound. You inflate the cuff until you can't hear the pulse, and deflate the cuff until it comes back, then you read the machine to see what the pressure is.

All of this was a lot to be doing on my first case, and the operation went on for a gruelling five hours, which is an extremely long time in which to stay clear and focused. When it goes on for that long you can usually find someone to take over for a few minutes so that you can stretch, go to the loo and eat something sustaining and quick, like a banana, but other than that you are expected to stay with your case for the whole time.

What makes it even harder is that the operating theatres are kept very warm. When an animal is under anaesthesia it can't control its body temperature and can become too cold and even hypothermic. The room is kept warm to counter that, but it has the unfortunate effect of making you feel extremely sleepy. By four hours in you're hungry, sleepy and praying it isn't going to take much longer.

The reason an operation like this takes so long is because to reach the lungs you must cut open the sternum with bone-cutters, and then wire it back together again at the end. It's a big procedure and fascinating to watch.

There are usually six or seven people in any operation; the anaesthetist clinician, the anaesthesia student (in this case, me), the head surgeon, resident surgeon (a vet training to be specialist surgeon) and two veterinary nurses. There is often also a student who isn't scrubbed in, who scribes, or writes up the operation notes.

Because it's a long time and everyone is concentrating, very little is said, which is perhaps why the students get quizzed so much; it keeps everyone alert.

At the end of every day, between 5 and 6pm, we students would sit around a table and discuss our current cases and the ones to come the next day. We'd be asked why we'd chosen certain drugs, what the dosage was, what the alternatives were, how the drugs would affect the heart and a dozen other questions. A senior anaesthetist was a formidable chap called Haidar, who had a reputation for being fierce and utterly relentless in his questioning. And he lived up to this. At the evening round-up he would sometimes grill one of us for half an hour at a time, before moving on to someone else.

We did discover, though, that there was another side to Haidar. Although his natural expression was rather grumpy and our first impression of him was terrifying (an impression he rather liked to cultivate, I suspect), he was often very funny, clowning around, joking and making us all laugh.

Haidar liked to sit in the hallway between the anaesthesia induction room and surgical theatres, ordering people around from his chair. He continually grumbled about the hot weather. We were all revelling in a rare sunny spell, but it brought no joy for Haidar. To everyone's surprise, though, what distracted him from his daily grumbles was the film crew. He rather liked having the cameras around when a scene was being filmed.

Towards the end of the first week it was Jacques' twenty-eitgth birthday, so I raced home after work to talk to him on Skype. Only ten more days and I would be flying out to

South Africa again. I was starting the trip with two weeks' work experience alongside some wildlife vets in the north of the country and I would see Jacques after that, when I would be spending a whole month with him, writing my research project and doing some more work experience with a vet friend of his. I couldn't wait. For his birthday I'd bought him a GoPro camcorder, which I was going to take out with me. I was looking forward to giving it to him, but for the moment all I could do was tell him how much I was missing him.

The week passed in a blur of operations, equipment trays, intubation and recording of vital signs, all the while struggling to stay focused in operations and being grilled by clinicians. The longest operation I was involved in was six hours on a retriever with a ruptured diaphragm, and the saddest was an operation on a boxer with an advanced mast cell tumour that could not be completely removed.

By Friday afternoon I was ready for a break, but before we went home we were called together by Haidar for what he referred to as a 'lucky dip', which was actually anything but lucky, since it involved him choosing us at random to answer questions. I was picked first and he asked me about anaesthetic plans for a pyometra, or infected womb. As I struggled through my answers he followed one question with another until I had been in the firing line for half of the hour-long lucky dip session.

By the end I felt as though I'd been under interrogation, but at least I'd survived.

'Rather you than me,' Lucy remarked as we were leaving the room. 'You did pretty well. I couldn't have answered some of those questions.'

'Thanks,' I said grimly. 'That was horrible. He picked on me for so long. I just kept thinking surely he would ask someone else a question soon. But it's amazing how much suddenly comes back to you when you're put under extreme duress. At least I know now that the information is in my brain somewhere. Maybe I'm like Sherlock Holmes with his mind palace.'

Lucy laughed. 'Just hope we all are. We're all going to be put on the spot like that at some point. And that's just the clinicians; after that we've got the exams.'

'Don't remind me,' I sighed. 'Can't even think about that yet.'

I went back to the house to catch up with James and John over a glass of wine. I would have loved to have gone home that weekend to see my parents and my horses, but I was on call on the Saturday and at three in the afternoon I was called in for an operation on a dachshund with a prolapsed disc. He was a lovely little dog, a black long-haired little chap called Butch, which I assumed was ironic. Poor Butch had lost the use of his hind legs and was incontinent, so he needed help.

A lot of dachshunds have genetic problems with their spines. Not surprising, perhaps, given their short legs and very long backs. A prolapsed or ruptured disc is quite common in the breed and very painful but it can be helped with surgery. It was a long and intricate operation, but by the time I left for home at nine o'clock that night Butch was fast asleep in a comfortable kennel in the ICU department and on his way to recovery.

At the start of my second week we had an equine seminar in which we were taught how to anaesthetise horses. I asked Haidar if I could do an equine case and the following day he sent me over to the Equine Centre to help with a stifle arthroscopy – keyhole surgery on the stifle joint in the horse's hind leg. Keyhole surgery with an arthroscope, performed under general anaesthetic, is becoming more common for horses with joint problems and the success rate is good.

I arrived early in the morning and had the chance to place my first venous catheter in a horse (a catheter or tube placed into the jugular vein in the horse's neck). I did it first time and was really pleased with myself. The catheter is used to attach the horse to plenty of fluids during surgery to keep its blood pressure up and to provide immediate intravenous access should we need to administer any emergency drugs.

It was a busy morning. I had to record even more information for the horse under anaesthetic than I had for smaller animals. I also had to take blood gases to measure the horse's heart function, but I felt awful because I spilt some blood into the blood gas analyser, a very delicate machine, and broke it. I apologised profusely, but there wasn't time to deal with it because the horse was still under.

The operation was a success, the horse was soon back on its feet and I was told not to worry about the machine – though I did, of course. But there wasn't a lot of time to feel bad about it because I had to rush back to the QMH to help with the complicated case of a Russian terrier, a huge dog a bit like a black bear, which had potentially fatal arrhythmia, or irregular heart beat. The clinicians were concerned that he had a mass, or possibly a clot, in his heart. It was a high-stress situation – no one was sure that the dog would pull through or what they were going to find, so we had plenty of crash drugs on hand and a portable defibrillator in case his heart stopped. But, almost miraculously, it went well. There was a clot, not a mass, it was removed and the dog recovered well. This was great news for the owners as things could have been far worse – the clot could easily have dislodged at any time and formed an embolism in the lungs, or blocked a large vessel. Or it could have been a cancerous mass in his heart.

In the second week the film crew turned their attention to me, but by then I was feeling more confident and beginning to get the hang of anaesthesia. The clinicians weren't quite as scary as their reputations had suggested, and in fact most of them were supportive and keen to teach. To my surprise, since I'd dreaded this rotation, I found that I was actually enjoying it.

The film crew with me this time were Amy, whom I already knew really well, and Rob – Scottish, in his twenties and so good looking that most of the females in the department fancied him. The nurses and other students would often whisper to me and Grace, out of his hearing, that they were jealous because we were filming with him. Rob acted as if he were oblivious, although we were all pretty sure he was well aware of the stir he was causing.

The agreement was that the film crews were not allowed to interfere in any way with the animals or with our work. They could set up shots such as walking down a corridor or sitting in the tea room, but when it came to the animals they had to simply observe and to remain as discreet as possible. In between cases, they would regularly round up a few of us and get us to walk down the corridor chatting about the day's work, although luckily we didn't have microphones on for those shots, as usually the conversation went along the lines of:

'I can't believe we're doing this again. We look like such idiots to all the staff in this hospital.'

'Do you think the general public will be able to lip-read what we're saying?'

'No, I'm sure if we keep these fake smiles plastered on they'll have no idea.'

'Quick, let's all do a fake laugh as if we're talking about something really funny.'

Towards the end of the second week, feeling bolder after a few successful cases, I asked Haidar to give me cases that would stretch me; ones that might be a little more complicated than others. And that's when he assigned me to Rover.

Rover was a tiny, sandy-coloured Chihuahua, who was almost as wide as he was high, with big, black eyes and a tongue that stuck out. At nine years old he wasn't young, he had a patch of greying fur around his muzzle and his eyes were a little cloudy.

Chihuahuas are the smallest breed of dog. Usually no more than eight or nine inches tall and weighing four or five pounds, they have huge eyes and enormous ears. Named after a state in Mexico, where the breed originates, they are classic 'handbag' dogs, but in fact, like all dogs, they need plenty of exercise and shouldn't be carried around.

Rover was very quiet, and he looked at me with big, sad eyes. Although I wasn't especially fond of 'handbag' breeds I felt very sorry for the poor little chap. He had been fishing with his owner and had snuffled up the bait. Unfortunately, the bait was on a fishhook, which he had also eaten. Now Rover needed surgery to remove the hook, which would otherwise almost certainly rupture his gastrointestinal tract and lead to septic shock, which would kill him.

I had a speedy read through his history and gave him a quick once-over to try to work out an anaesthetic plan. The Spanish anaesthetist in charge, Julio, was expecting me to tell him exactly what, when and how much anaesthetic we should be giving Rover. However, Rover had a real complication, in the form of the loudest heart murmur I had ever heard. Anaesthetic drugs have a profound effect on the heart, so Rover's anaesthesia would have to be short and involve drugs I wasn't used to using. The likelihood of his heart stopping was high.

I relayed my plan to Julio, and after a quick quizzing about how the drugs worked, during which I actually surprised myself with the answers that popped out of my mouth, he agreed with my choice.

I went to collect Rover from the Emergency Room, where he was waiting, to bring him to the induction room. I picked him up in my arms, giving him a gentle cuddle. Once he was on the table Julio and I first had to sedate him with an injection into the vein in his front leg, in which he already had a catheter. After that we slowly induced him into anaesthesia – at which point he stopped breathing. It was a rush to get the delicate intubation tube down his very tiny windpipe to connect him to the anaesthetic machine so we could give him some breaths. I had to twist and push while taking great care not to injure him. We were clearly in for a tough time if we were to keep him stable.

As soon as he was breathing for himself again, we wheeled him quickly down the corridor to the operating room. There's an unwritten rule that if an animal is being wheeled down the corridor, everyone flattens against the wall to make way. As we whizzed along with Rover, people leaped out of our way. I was grateful for the rule – we didn't have a minute to spare.

We only had one shot at removing the fishhook, and that would be by putting an endoscope (a fibre-optic camera) down his throat so that we could see exactly what was happening. The hook would then need to be gently removed.

The minimum amount of anaesthesia is used in a case like this, where there are potential heart complications, and the move had caused Rover to start waking up. A small top-up of anaesthetic was given to him intravenously, which sent him back to sleep but again caused him to cease breathing. He was proving difficult to manage; either the anaesthetic was too light and he was waking up, or it was far too deep and he was not breathing. After a short struggle to get him to a more stable anaesthesia depth, the two senior clinicians of the small animal medicine department, Hattie Syme and Chris Scudder, came to perform the endoscopy.

Chris slowly started inserting the endoscope down Rover's throat and we all gazed at the screen as the camera showed us what was happening.

'Ah,' Chris said calmly. 'The hook's not in his oesophagus. It's actually stuck through the oesophagus wall.' There was an eerie silence in the room. Not a sound, apart from the bleeps from the anaesthetic machine. We all knew that the risk factor had just trebled. Getting a hook out of the delicate wall of the oesophagus would be incredibly hard; the risk of tearing the oesophagus was considerable, and that would be fatal.

After a long pause Hattie spoke up. 'Well, if you don't get that hook out, the only place this dog is going is to heaven.' We all knew it was true, but her words still felt shocking.

Over the next ten minutes, the tension in the room could have been cut with a knife. Everyone was feeling it as we watched the screen intently. Chris had inserted a small pair of forceps and was very gently wiggling away at the hook, trying to cause as little extra damage as possible. Finally, to an audible sigh of relief, it slipped out of the oesophagus wall and we could see the whole thing on the screen. It was a big hook for such a small dog.

The next step was as tense as the first. The hook had to be brought up without scraping against the throat, or being dropped. Chris passed a soft tube down Rover's throat and then gently and slowly manoeuvred the fishhook into it and pulled out the tube – and the hook. As it came out the room erupted into cheers. He had done it.

Back in the induction room Julio and I waited patiently for Rover to wake up. The anaesthetist's role wasn't finished until the patient was fully awake and back to normal. The cameras were still following us, and Rob asked us how we felt. Still a little emotional, I said, 'We saved a life today.' Julio roared with laughter and I turned pink. I hadn't meant to sound quite so corny, but it was true – Rover had come perilously close to dying, and he was still with us, minus the hook. It was an overwhelming feeling, knowing that the team's skill had saved him.

When it came to writing his formal feedback on my performance in anaesthesia, Julio put, 'She's a TV superstar.' He thought the whole thing was hilarious.

I was keen to get away early on our last Friday because I was flying to South Africa the next day, but we weren't going to escape without another 'lucky dip' interrogation, this time from Julio. He was a little softer on us than Haidar had been and we brought in cakes, which smoothed the way, so there was a bit more banter and a bit less grilling.

I had all my luggage in my car, so after saying goodbye to everyone in anaesthesia and to Lucy and the girls in my group, whom I wouldn't be seeing for the next six weeks, I headed for Kent, hoping to spend the evening catching up with everyone at home. That plan went out of the window when a bomb scare on the Dartford crossing out of London stopped the traffic. I spent the evening in my car, with no supper, and didn't get back until midnight.

On Saturday morning I rushed into town to get my international driving licence. I was flying to Johannesburg that night and meeting two other vet students, one from Poland and one from Germany, at the airport on Sunday morning. I'd arranged a hire car and we were going to drive up to Kruger together, to begin our placement early on Monday.

With the licence sorted I went over to the stables to give both the horses a ride out. I was so pleased to see them but, unbelievably, they'd got fatter! I spent a couple of hours with them, gave them a goodbye nuzzle and went home to pack. And that's when the text arrived from British Airways to say that my flight had been postponed until the following day.

I was totally thrown. If I didn't get there on Sunday morning the other two vet students, Natalia and Tina, would be stuck at the airport for twenty-four hours waiting for me, because the hire car was in my name. Dad got on the line to BA, but two hours and several calls later he'd had no luck.

'Right, let's drive up to Heathrow and we'll find you a flight there,' he announced. Mum said she'd come, too, so we piled my bags into the car, I said goodbye to Ross and we headed for the airport, where Dad managed to get me transferred to a Virgin flight leaving only an hour later. I was so relieved I burst into tears at the desk and then felt horribly embarrassed.

After a quick dinner and a change of terminal I said a tearful goodbye to my parents and was on my way to the departure gate when I bumped into Grace, on her way to New Zealand to spend a couple of weeks working with farm vets.

'Sheep?' I asked.

'Mostly cows, actually.'

My flight was being called. 'I have to go. Enjoy the cows. See you in a few weeks.'

As I hurtled off she waved and called after me. 'Don't sweat it with the lions. And have fun.'

CHAPTER NINE

Into the Wild

As I made my way through the terminal, with its brightly decorated walls and the morning sun streaming in through the windows, I felt the buzz of being in Africa again.

I spotted the two vet students straight away and went over to say hello. Natalia was Polish, tall with long, dark hair and rather shy and quiet, while Tina, from Germany, was short, blonde, a non-stop talker and a bit of a rocker, her eyes circled in dark liner.

I sorted the paperwork for the car and we set off. Natalia didn't drive, so Tina and I had agreed to share the five- or six-hour journey between us. I drove first and I was grateful for Tina, chatting away beside me and keeping me awake. At the halfway point we switched and I climbed into the back to try to get some sleep.

The three of us were there courtesy of the veterinary services for a northern game reserve. We'd been lucky to get the placements because the veterinary services only took on international students once they had placed all their own South African students.

Our destination was a small village based inside the reserve where the vets were based, along with a cluster of tourist huts and a village for all the reserve staff, complete with church, school and swimming pool.

It was nice to view a few animals on the drive through the park to the village, especially since I had taken over driving again.

When we arrived, hot and dusty but thankfully in one piece, we were shown to the guest accommodation, which was tucked in between the clinic and the staff village. We had a bedroom each, opening onto a patch of grass that we had to cross to get to the showers. The kitchen was an open tent, with a table at one end. We would therefore be enjoying a lot of alfresco living, but with the warm, dry South African days and nights, that was fine with us – although, unlike the tourist villages, the staff village and our accommodation had no fencing around it to keep the wildlife out.

The team included three wildlife vets, another vet training to be a wildlife specialist and a number of ground staff, including an anaesthetist and several technicians, plus extra staff to help haul the larger animals in and out of trucks and crates. And, of course, we three eager but uninitiated trainee vets.

After an outdoor supper of boerwors, a South African

beef sausage that's absolutely delicious, and a chat with Natalia and Tina, I was in bed by 8pm, absolutely wiped out after my twenty hours of travelling.

The following morning the three of us turned up at the clinic at 7.30am ready to get stuck in, only to be told by Gale, the head vet technician, that it was going to be a quiet day. He showed us around the clinic, a large building full of offices, labs and storage rooms, and the pens and bomas that held the inpatients inside. Once we'd looked around, Gale told us that that there was nothing for us to do until the hyena capture that night, so we went off for a game drive.

No matter how many times I see wildlife in their natural habitat, I still feel absolute awe. On our three-hour drive we spotted buffalo, giraffe, zebra, impala, warthog, elephant, rhino and cheetah. All of them living free, in the wide open spaces and natural beauty of the park.

When we got back we had a swim before reporting back to the clinic at 4pm to help pack the pickup trucks, known as bakkies. We were going out to try to capture a few hyenas, hopefully five or six of them, for research purposes. The vets wanted to find out whether hyenas carry tuberculosis. Hyenas have never produced clinical cases of TB but as scavengers they feed on the remains of carcasses – including the lungs – of animals that have TB, so the suspicion was that they might well be carriers.

We met two of the vets: Dr Pretorius, the senior vet in charge, and Dr Jenny, a qualified vet training to be a wildlife specialist. Dr Pretorius was tall and deeply tanned, with a full head of white hair. He was friendly, but at the same time you had a feeling that it would be better not to cross him. Dr Jenny was tall with curly brown hair and she was extremely easy to talk to. Vets in South Africa are all treated with great respect and addressed as Doctor, so once qualified I would be Dr Hardy, or Dr Jo. I quite fancied that idea.

When everything was on board the pickups we were told to climb into the open back of one of them. Hyenas are more active at night, and in any case it wouldn't be possible to dart them with curious tourists around. So as the sun was setting, and after the 6pm curfew for tourists, we set out for a spot where a group of hyenas had been seen. Strictly speaking the collective name for a group of hyenas is a cackle, which makes you want to, well, cackle. And for rhinos it's a crash, while for giraffes it's a tower, for buffalo it's a gang and for hippos it's a bloat. Who knew? The only one I was familiar with was a pride of lions.

Anyway, several trucks set out in convoy for a known hyena den, but we found nothing there, so we moved to a more open spot where, through speakers on top of one of the trucks, we played the distress sounds of warthog and buffalo, hoping to trick the hyenas into thinking that something in this area would be easy prey. It was pitch dark and we sat in silence with the lights off, our eyes straining for any signs of hyena. I really didn't like the noises, which did actually sound very distressed.

Twenty minutes passed, then thirty, with no sign of any hyenas. Off we went again, to another clearing a few miles away where hyena had been spotted earlier. Out went the lights and the distress sounds were played again. After five minutes we picked up the distant whooping of hyenas. But they didn't come any closer. Sound alone wasn't enough; they were waiting for the scent of prey.

A couple of brave helpers offered to get out and tie some meat to the tailgate. While they were doing that, it was everyone else's responsibility to keep a lookout. When they were done the men dived back into the truck and the driver did a few laps of the clearing to spread the scent. They then got out again and tied the meat to a pole sticking out in front of the truck. All the lights were turned off again, the distress noises were played and the whooping came closer. They had to be within a few hundred metres of the trucks, but none of the torches were on so we couldn't tell for sure, until, suddenly, two large shadows swooped so close to the truck I was in that I jumped. The hyenas had arrived.

We gave it a couple of minutes to make sure they had taken the bait and then the headlights were switched on to reveal four startled hyenas, standing right in front of us. Dr

Pretorius fired two darts and they scattered into the bush. He was confident that he had hit two of them and we were told to get out and help the assistants find them.

Only later did it dawn on me exactly what he had been asking of us; to go out into the pitch black into the African bush, with hyenas, lions and leopards all around, not to mention deadly snakes, to find two hyenas that might or might not actually be asleep.

Still, all in a day's work, and we did find them both about twenty-five metres into the thick bush. Between several of us we hauled them onto stretchers then carried them out of the undergrowth and loaded them onto the back of a waiting truck. Tina, Natalia and I were told to get in beside them and to watch them to make sure they kept breathing and didn't wake up.

Two was a good start, but Dr Pretorius wanted more, so again we were plunged into pitch darkness for a re-run of the bait and distress sounds scenario. Except that this time the three of us were in the open back of a pickup with two sleeping hyenas. Looking back on it, I don't know why I wasn't nervous. But at the time we were completely absorbed in the tension and excitement of what was happening.

Shadows flitted past, as the hyenas that had dispersed returned. Suddenly, the lights flashed on and Dr Pretorius darted a third hyena. The assistants went and found it and put it on the back of the truck beside the two that were already sleeping.

By that time it was eleven at night and it was decided that, as the first two had now been under for around an hour and the anaesthetic would soon begin to wear off, we should get them back to base to take some samples. So we set off, Dr Jenny with us and Dr Pretorius in the truck behind us. Because hyenas are big creatures and we were sitting in an area not much bigger than a dining table, we were practically on top of them and, as the bakkie rattled along the dirt road at 50 mph, we clung to the sides and tried not to fall on the hyenas. We continued to check that all three were well under but still breathing; every few minutes we listened to see if their hearts were steady and then we turned on our torches to see if they were alright – not easy when jolting along a dirt road.

Twenty minutes later we pulled up at the gate of the clinic. We had to wait for Dr Pretorius, as he had the keys to the complex, but his truck was nowhere to be seen or even heard. Dr Jenny told us not to worry and said that he had probably just got caught up somewhere, possibly with something like an elephant crossing the road. We'd just wait until he returned.

Suddenly Tina yelped. 'Jo, look, the one beside you is moving its tongue.'

I peered down at it, and then tried its blink reflex by

tapping the corner of an eye. It blinked. This hyena was waking up! And we had no top-up drugs with us to put it back under; all we had were our stethoscopes and torches.

I told Dr Jenny, who phoned Dr Pretorius. He had stopped to dart another hyena, and was going to be a further five minutes. As she came off the phone, the hyena was starting to move its head. Dr Jenny told me to lie on it and pin its head down. So I did. I had my hands on its neck, pinning down its head with my arms while trying to keep my head out of the way.

Bearing in mind that hyenas are the strongest of all mammals, with 2,000 pounds of pressure per square inch to their bite, I wouldn't have stood a chance if it had woken fully and decided it didn't appreciate someone lying on top of it. I should have been leaping out of the truck and running in the opposite direction, but as the hyena began to move its head a little more and its legs twitched, Dr Pretorius finally arrived and dived out of his truck and into the back of ours, syringe in hand. Seconds later, to my immense relief, the hyena was out cold again.

Dr Pretorius had the fourth hyena sprawled across the back seat of his truck. Once the gate was unlocked, we drove them into the clinic and unloaded them off the bakkies. Given that they weighed upwards of 110 pounds each, it took several of us to lift each one, but eventually all four were inside. We took blood, did skin TB tests and performed BALs (broncho-aveolar lavages – aka lung washes) on each of them. A lung wash shows the types of cells within the lung and this can give clues as to whether the animal has healthy lungs and if not, what kind of disease the lungs were reacting to. The blood test, called a Bovigam test, indicates if the animal has had any previous or current immune reaction to TB, and a skin TB test shows whether the body has been exposed to TB previously. Antigen is injected and if the skin swells up over the next few days on the injection site, it's a positive reaction, which indicates that the body recognises the antigen because it has TB, or has had it in the past. When we finished we put them into cages and woke them up. The plan was to keep them for a couple of days to see the results of the skin TB tests, after which they would be released into the wild again, back at the place where we had found them.

After processing the BAL and blood samples in the on-site lab we were finished for the night. By the time I got into bed it was almost two in the morning. The hyena capture had been amazing, and as I drifted off to sleep I began to think that wildlife work could be something I would really consider as a career.

After several more nights spent capturing hyenas, in week two we turned our attention to rhinos. The clinic does a lot of conservation work, and they hoped, over the following couple of weeks, to move sixty rhinos out of this section of the park, where they were regularly being poached, to a much safer area a day's drive away. This meant capturing the rhinos and transporting them on trucks, so they also planned to take blood from each rhino and do a basic health screening at the same time.

Rhino poaching is a very serious problem in South Africa. Over the previous year 1,200 rhinos had been killed by poachers who hunt them for their horns, which are sold on the black market for as much as gold. This is a 21 per cent increase on the previous year, and a horrifying 9,300 per cent increase from 2007. Asian countries, Vietnam and China in particular, prize the horns for their medicinal and aphrodisiac purposes.

There are two species of rhino, black and white. All are in fact exactly the same dark grey-brown, with a thick skin that looks like armour. The key difference between them is lip shape; the term 'white' is believed to have come from the Afrikaans word *wyd*, which refers to the rhino's square upper lip. They are grazers and live in open areas. Black rhinos have hooked lips to pick leaves off bushes, and they are more rarely seen as they're often hidden among the vegetation. Enormous creatures, weighing up to a tonne each, they are vegetarian and roam the grasslands of just four African countries: South Africa, Namibia, Zimbabwe and Kenya. Eighty per cent of all rhinos are found in South

Africa, and half of these, around 10,000, are in Kruger National Park, a park about the same size as Israel. Huge efforts are made by the government and wildlife services to combat poaching, but the poachers are clever and determined, so staying ahead of them is a challenge.

Moving a rhino is not easy. It needs to be done in the cool of the morning, because once under anaesthetic animals can't regulate their body heat, and in the scorching midday sun the rhinos could overheat and die. So we set off each morning at three, a couple of hours before sunrise, a convoy of bakkies with about a dozen of us crammed into the back of each, along with ropes and vast crates. At that time in the morning it was really cold, but we knew that by 10am it would be baking hot, so we had to dress in layers, shedding them as the sun came up.

We looked for the rhino close to the perimeter of the park, where they were most vulnerable to poachers. It was about an hour's drive for us to get there, and once we'd found them a helicopter with a vet on board would come and join us, and the vet would dart the rhino from the helicopter. The rhino, shocked by the noise and the dart, began to run and we'd follow it until it came to a halt about three minutes later. It's vital to find the rhino once they've been darted as unconscious they're completely defenceless and can easily be attacked by lions or hyenas. So if the rhino headed for bush that was too dense to drive through, the helicopter would fly low, trying to push them towards the road.

By the time we caught up with the rhino it would still be attempting to run, lifting one leg after the other but staying on the spot, unable to move forward. At that point every-one on the trucks sprang into action. One of the team would throw a blindfold over the rhino and the whole team would push it over onto its side. That was the cue for Tina, Natalia and me to grab our equipment trays and sample bottles and get going. We needed to take ten different tubes of blood for various tests. By the end of the week we were really good at hitting rhino veins. You can try an ear, but often the blood pressure there isn't very good, so it's better to try a vein deep in the leg. You have to do it completely blind by feeling a dip in between two bones on the inside of the leg, below its knee, and then plunging in the needle.

We also had to get faecal samples, which meant putting a gloved hand in the rectum to get out some matter and filling a sample pot. Then we'd take a tissue sample, by cutting off a tiny slither of skin on the ear and sprinkling cauterizing powder over it to stop it bleeding. And finally we had to take a hair sample, by plucking some hairs from the tail.

While the three of us were taking all the samples, another team was drilling holes in the horns and putting in microchips, and a third team was putting on ropes so that once the samples were taken we could wake the rhino enough to get it back onto its feet and walk it into a large metal crate that a fourth team would have waiting.

All of this took place in under two minutes, with the vets yelling at us to hurry up and our fingers slipping on the syringes as we raced against the clock. It is vital that rhinos don't stay under too long; they are so heavy that their weight can stop the blood supply to their legs and if that happens, you can't get them up again.

We'd divide the jobs between us – 'You get the faecal sample, you do the ear, I'll do the blood' – but sometimes two rhinos were darted at once, perhaps a mother and calf or two sister rhinos grazing together, and we'd have to split up, one of us taking one rhino, the other two taking the second. While we took all the samples, the vets and technicians would be monitoring the anaesthetic and drilling holes in the horns to insert microchips into them in case the rhinos were poached for that part of their body.

If we got everything done in time the vets would allow us to administer the reversal drug to wake the rhino. Ropes and pulleys would be thrown around it, and it would take at least ten or twelve of us to get it upright and then push and pull it into the crate. Once in, the rhino would be given the remainder of the antidote to fully wake it, and then a small crane would lift the crate onto a lorry.

At one point, when we'd darted two rhinos at once, the

team had a problem getting the first into the crate, which meant that the second lay unconscious on its side for an extra five minutes. To keep the blood supply to the legs going, Dr Jenny and I had to take a back leg each and pump them up and down. The legs were incredibly heavy and it was hard work moving them at all, let alone pumping, but knowing the damage that would happen if we didn't, we heaved and pushed until it was time to wake the rhino.

We went through this routine every day for a week and caught thirty-five rhinos; an excellent tally. It was a wonderful thing to work so closely with these extraordinary creatures who look prehistoric and whose history goes back fourteen million years.

Our adventures in the bush were not without incident. At one point, as I sat on the side of a bakkie, trying desperately not to fall off while we were off-roading through the bush, a tree branch swiped my back, cutting my strappy top in half and slicing right across my skin. It hurt, but we had nothing to put on it, so I just had to put up with it. And as I didn't have another top with me I spent the rest of the morning in half a top. I found it quite embarrassing as we had some investors with us who had been allowed to come and experience the work the clinic did, and so we had our guests around us, photographing what the team were doing, and there was I, trying to stay out of shot with my battered top and bleeding back.

The second incident was a little more alarming. The drug used to dart the rhinos, called M99, was opioid-based and fatal to humans, so we were told never to touch the dart or the site of the dart; all of this had to be done by experienced people. The technicians would often be the ones to pull the dart out of the animal using a Leatherman, a metal multi-tool a bit like a Swiss army knife, and put it in a sealed container for the vets to dispose of later.

On the third day I was taking faecal samples from a rhino, with one hand on the rhino's back, when a technician pulled the dart out of the rhino's side, accidentally grazing the back of my hand with it. Dr Pretorius was jumping in and out of the helicopter at that point, so I ran to Gale, the head technician. There was a red mark on the back of my hand and I didn't know whether any of the drug might have been left on the dart, so I felt very scared. Gale was calm and collected. He told me to wash my hand and then let him know if I felt strange in any way, sleepy or dizzy. There was a reversal drug, called M5050, but to give it without having absorbed any M99 would have nasty side effects.

Gale was experienced, I trusted him, and in any case there wasn't much else I could do. I felt nervous for the next couple of hours, but despite my close shave I was fine. I phoned Jacques that evening to tell him what had happened. He was well aware of the dangers of wildlife work, having spent a year in a game capture team before I met him. He was fuming at the technician who had grazed my hand, and for once I was glad he wasn't with me as he could be fiercely protective and a little hot-headed.

The second week sped by and suddenly it was time to go. On our last night we went for drinks beside a beautiful dam just outside the staff village. It was a breathtaking spot, well away from the tourist track. As we sat under a tree, watching the sun go down and sipping our sundowners with a few of the staff, Natalia, Tina and I toasted an unforgettable two weeks.

The next day we drove back to Johannesburg and said our goodbyes. Natalia and Tina headed home and I flew to Port Elizabeth for a long-anticipated reunion with Jacques. After almost five months apart, seeing him again was very emotional. And this time we would have a whole month together.

CHAPTER TEN

Between Two Worlds

My month with Jacques, working, lazing and finishing off my research, had been blissful. Now, though, the wide-open plains and the colours and scents of Africa seemed so far away. I wouldn't be going back again until after my finals, the following summer. I sighed. I had so much work to get through before then that the thought of it made my head spin.

As yet another apparently lame horse was paraded in front of us, my thoughts drifted back to Africa. It had been lovely to be back at Madolos, where Michael and the ladies – Helezin, Patricia and Valencia – greeted me warmly. Jacques and I planned to spend a week or so there before taking a road trip to Johannesburg, to see his family and attend his friend's wedding.

A couple of days after I arrived I felt tired and all my muscles hurt. Jacques, recognising the symptoms, made me go to a doctor. I had my second dose of tick-bite fever, this time from a minute pepper tick bite on my foot, no doubt picked up in the bush while working on my wildlife placement. Tick-bite fever can be really nasty, as I knew from my previous encounter four years earlier, but I was lucky and after a few days on antibiotics I felt much better, if still pretty tired.

Before we set off on the fifteen-hour drive to Johannesburg, Jacques suggested we stop on the way to camp for a couple of nights in Mountain Zebra National Park and I jumped at the idea. I loved going to new places and Jacques, with his detailed knowledge of animals and plants, was the perfect guide.

Named after the Cape Mountain zebra, the park at first appears a little disappointing; vast, open and flat, a valley between two mountains, with very little wildlife. It's only when you drive to the top that you discover a huge plain there, with stunning views all around and a wealth of animal life.

We pitched our tent in time to watch the sunset with a glass of wine, just as two zebra stallions started a fight. Jacques whipped out his camera to capture the tussle, etched against the setting sun. It was so beautifully romantic that I hoped Jacques might think it was the perfect spot in which to propose. He'd already missed so many opportunities to go down on one knee in some gorgeous, romantic spot over the past year, surely he was going to get around to it soon? Goodness knows I'd been dropping enough hints. But once again he missed his chance, and I had to settle for the sunset and the wine.

On to Johannesburg and a warm welcome from Jacques' parents, Elna and Johan. I've known them since my first summer in South Africa when he and I were just friends, so I never had to go through the toe-curling 'this is my girl-friend' introduction. They live in a suburb of the city, in a house that is pristine. Elna is an interior designer, and like Jacques' younger sister Sonia, she's chatty and affectionate and has always treated me like one of the family. Johan, who works for a company that manufactures cranes, is more reserved, but he's actually very kind and very protective of his family.

I always enjoy spending time with Sonia. She lives in the city, works in the legal world and she brings out my girly side. She wears lovely clothes, does her nails beautifully and always looks good, while I spend most of my time with hair pulled back and nails clipped short. Being a vet and looking elegant just don't go together. But within an hour or two of getting together with Sonia, I'm talking fashion and hair, and loving it.

That weekend Jacques' friend Jason was getting married to his long-time girlfriend, Laura. It was going to be a big do and I was looking forward to my first South African wedding, which turned out to be just like an

English wedding in some ways, but completely different in others.

Take the traditional heckling of the groom by his closest friends, including Jacques, of course.

When the time came for his speech, Jason stood up and began a romantic and emotional speech about the bride. Praising her beauty, describing how he fell in love with her, moving the guests almost to tears. Until his friends pulled up their chairs in a semicircle in front of him and began whistling, heckling and cat-calling.

He struggled on, doing his best to ignore the cacophony, and eventually, to cheers and stamps, he got to the end of his speech. After which the whole room leaped to their feet and began to whirl and spin in a sokkie, the dance that all Afrikaners love – a mix of ballroom and jive that's fast, fun and furious.

Most Afrikaner men can dance sokkie and know how to lead their partners, and Jacques is no exception. In fact, his dancing is one of the things that made me fall for him; I love to dance with someone who can lead me effortlessly through a series of spins, turns and lifts. And because he's tall, I can wear my highest heels (which make me over six foot, since I'm five-eight in my socks) and he still towers over me.

We danced until we dropped, and then spent another couple of days with Jacques' family, relaxing and catching up with the rugby – a national obsession that Jacques and his dad share with most of the South African population.

We drove back to Madolos in a day and while Jacques got back to work I spent a few days writing up my research project. Jacques was also working on some research for his Masters, a study of the way rodent populations differ according to the varied plant life in game reserves, so we were able to talk it over and give each other a bit of support and advice.

The next day I went over to see my old friend Thys. He and Johma welcomed me warmly and sat me down in their kitchen for a coffee and an enormous slab of cake.

Thys asked me if I wanted to come and dart some buffalo with him, and of course I said yes.

He told me we were going to test the buffalo for Foot and Mouth Disease. The game reserve's owners wanted their herds certified free of FMD, which meant they would fetch a much higher price when they were sold. So off we went in his jeep, with Thys, as ever, pondering philosophical puzzles about the origins of life as we headed into the reserve.

Thys had roped in a team of helpers from the reserve staff, and they rounded up eight buffalo and put them into a livestock enclosure known as a boma. We darted them all and the second they were out cold we began taking blood samples from the jugular vein in the neck. After this, we started reversing the anaesthetics. After the rhino work I had just done I was used to working under pressure, but with my last buffalo I just couldn't find the vein in its ear to administer the reversal drug. I kept missing and I still hadn't managed it when the first buffalo began waking up.

'Come on, Englishman, hurry up,' Thys shouted, as I finally got the needle in. I drew back the plunger to check I was in the vein, and to my relief some blood flashed back into my syringe, so I pressed down the plunger and then sprinted out of the boma.

'Just in time then,' he said, and roared with laughter. Like so many of the vets working with wildlife, he thrived on the nail-biting moments.

Our next task was to move a delinquent adolescent rhino to the other section of the reserve. The rhino was still grazing with his mother, although he was old enough to leave her and, like a typical teenager, he was causing trouble by damaging the various small huts and wooden buildings across the reserve. Once he was darted, Thys shooed the mother off – on foot. How he managed to send her packing without getting flattened I'm not sure; rhino are huge but they can be surprisingly fast, and if one turns on you then you don't have a lot of time to make your escape. Somehow, Thys persuaded this mum to back off, and although she came back a couple of times Thys and the rest of the team waved her away each time.

The young rhino was out cold when Thys realised he didn't have a blindfold to put over the animal's head. You need to keep the animal in the dark, otherwise the light can wake it if the anaesthetic is not deep. Undaunted, Thys got a towel out of the back of the car and sellotaped it over the rhino's head, before giving him half the reversal drug. Then the team got him on his feet, threw ropes around him and hauled him onto the trailer while I videoed the scene. Thys loved to film his work and he would often shove his video camera into my hands with the words, 'Englishman, have the camera.' He'd expect me to record whatever he was doing, and he would film me when I was at work, too, as in the scenario with the boar castrations.

Thys decided not to wake the rhino fully until we reached its destination on the other side of the river that ran through the reserve. But when we reached the other side we realised that the trailer the rhino was in was more like a horse-box, and it had no window through which Thys could reach to administer the second half of the reversal drug. So, being Thys, he decided he would get into the trailer with the rhino, while he insisted I carried on filming, although I made sure I stayed at a distance. He nipped in, gave the injection, whipped off the blindfold and sprinted out, leaving the door open for the rhino to leave the box, which it did, hard on his heels.

The following day we were back on farms, inoculating cattle against heart water, a nasty tick-born parasitic infection that can lay waste to livestock herds. It's not present in the UK, but it is devastating in Africa. Thys used a primitive vaccine made from the blood of infected animals. It's injected and then three days later followed up with antibiotics. He kept his vaccine in heavy old metal canisters filled with dry ice. Once he'd used the vaccine he took the lid off my water bottle, stuffed in some dry ice and threw it across the yard, where it exploded like a bomb. He thought this was hilarious and made several more bottle-bombs, roaring with laughter as they exploded across the yard.

Thys was an extraordinary character; a talented vet, a passionate philosopher, a dare-devil and a schoolboy all rolled into one leather-skinned, white-haired, unconventional old man. Every time I worked with him he made me laugh, shocked me, stretched me to the limit and taught me invaluable lessons.

After an action-packed month in South Africa it was time to go home again. I arrived back in England on a bleak day in early November. I had a weekend with my family before driving back to college to prepare for my next rotation – equine orthopaedics.

On my first day the sky was grey and drizzly rain was making everything feel damp and chilly in the way that only a November day can be. In these unappealing conditions we were greeted with the news that we'd be spending most of our week outside, testing horses for lameness.

The thrill of this had worn thin by the end of the first hour.

'So what do you think about this horse? Is it lame or not?' The clinician fixed me with an icy glare.

I rubbed my arms and shivered as I looked at the horse being lunged in a circle in front of me. It looked absolutely fine.

'It's lame,' I said. 'In, er, the left foreleg? No, the right hind. Oh wait, erm, both? Maybe?'

'I think you'll find its lame in three legs. The left fore, the right hind, and the left hind.'

Really?

The horse didn't look lame; indeed its gait barely looked uneven. But the clinician wasn't finished.

'To what degree do you think it's lame? Lucy?'

'Oh, um, two-tenths?'

'Actually, just under one-tenth. Maybe a tiny bit more in that left foreleg. Since there are multiple lame limbs, the best way to start the diagnostic process is to bone-scan the horse. You students really must learn to spot lameness with more accuracy.'

Lucy and I looked at one another. I was beginning to think we were being played, and I could see she thought so, too. It was honestly impossible to see how the horse could be lame, let alone in three legs. I thought I was pretty good at spotting lameness, but I clearly still had some things to learn.

Lameness is measured on a scale of ten, with one-tenth being barely visible lameness. Anything under that wouldn't usually cause any concern; in fact, some people argue that lameness under one-tenth doesn't even exist, but the clinician clearly wanted to keep us on our toes, hence the 'Is this horse lame or not?' routine. We went through this performance at the Equine Centre endless times, watching horses that appeared to be pretty sound, while standing out in the rain – it rained for the entire week – and wishing we could be almost anywhere but there.

The only bright spot in the week was when we were told a case was coming in the following day for patella ligament surgery and I managed to bag it – anything for a break from the lameness routine. An hour later I went out to the car park to find an enormous lorry waiting there. Judging by its size it contained a very large horse, but as the door opened what emerged was a little skewbald (brown and white) Shetland pony, Otis, with more hair than body. He reminded me of the Thelwell cartoon ponies.

I introduced myself to his owner, Mrs Harris, and while she closed the lorry I took off Otis's travel boots, which were much too big for him and made him look like a toddler in grown-up wellies.

Otis may have been small, but he was a big personality. He strode into the barn and made himself instantly at home as the rest of the rotation group gathered round to say hello while I went with Tim, the clinician in charge, to take a detailed history from Mrs Harris.

Otis had a condition in which one of his back legs would lock in an extended position. Known as locking stifles, this happens when one of the ligaments holding the patella (kneecap) in place is slightly too long and sometimes gets caught over the end of the femur. It usually unlocks by itself after thirty seconds or so, but it can be quite distressing for the horse. Exercise to build up hind limb muscles often helps, but as Otis was too small to be ridden it was difficult for Mrs Harris to give him enough extra exercise, so he needed surgery.

Tim and I waved Mrs Harris off, and he told me to let my rotation group know we would be doing the surgery straight after lunch. I got back to the stable to find Lucy beaming and Otis with a catheter successfully placed in his neck. She had managed to insert it first time, proving that she wasn't half as bad at horsy stuff as she thought she was.

I peered over the stable door. Jade and Katy were giving Otis's voluminous mane a brush, while Grace talked soothingly to him in preparation for his operation. I dragged them all away for a quick lunch before we gathered at the knock-down box next to the surgical theatre where Tim, an equine nurse, a resident equine vet and an anaesthetist joined us. Otis was sedated and then given the ketamine–diazepam combination to knock him out. After a few seconds he fell gracefully to his knees and then onto his side with a small grunt. At least he didn't have far to fall!

After scrubbing in Tim located the ligament using an ultrasound machine and, with a very small scalpel, made several stabs along the length of the ligament. The idea was that when these cuts healed they would form scar tissue that would shorten the ligament and stop it catching. It was a simple operation and in minutes we were done. Twenty minutes later Otis was conscious again and attempting to stand. He was going to have a sore leg for a while; he wasn't going to be allowed pain relief since all equine pain relief is anti-inflammatory, and the whole point of the surgery was to create inflammation and scarring. I felt very sorry for him, but a day or two later he was well enough to go home and was loaded back into the huge lorry he had arrived in. Over the next few weeks it would become apparent whether the surgery had worked.

Little Otis proved to be our only bright spot that week. After the excitement and adventure of the wildlife work, trying to spot lameness in horses that looked perfectly fit was pretty dull. I was missing Jacques, and the sun, badly. And to make matters worse, the Saturday at the end of that week was my birthday. I would have loved to have been spending it with Jacques, but a Skype call would have to do. I wasn't even sure I'd manage the day off; we were expected to do weekend shifts, but at the last minute I managed to swap my shift that day and race home.

As it was just after bonfire night we had a houseful of uncles, aunts, cousins and grandparents, a buffet and fireworks. After the week I'd had I was more than ready to party, so it was nice to catch up with everyone and it made a welcome break.

The following week we were back at the equine centre for equine soft-tissue surgery, which was a lot more interesting than the orthopaedics. It meant an early start at the stables to do our SOAP – Subjective, Objective, Assessment and Plan – for each horse we'd been assigned to, checking to see if it was bright, alert and responsive, checking its pulses, gum colour, heart-rate, gut sounds, breathing rate and temperature, and generally assessing whether it was improving or deteriorating. After that we had to decide what we thought should be done; more or less drugs, different drugs, diagnostic tests and so on.

We had to get out of the way by 8.30am, when the clinicians did their rounds, so we'd slope off to have breakfast before meeting the clinicians to go through our findings. This usually involved a grilling along the lines of, 'Fine, but have you thought of this?' or 'Why do you think that would help?'

My first patient was an event horse called Mackenzie. He hadn't been performing well, was breathing noisily and wheezing, and we needed to find out why.

He was a handsome fellow, chestnut with white markings, and he stood at least seventeen hands high, which is five feet eight inches at his withers – the point where his neck meets his back – meaning that the top of my head was just about level with his nose.

We suspected that Mackenzie had RLN, or recurrent laryngeal neuropathy, a condition in which the top of the windpipe is partially closed because the nerve that supplies signals from the brain to the larynx, called the recurrent laryngeal nerve, has been damaged in some way. This is easily done, as the nerve takes a tortuous route from the brain, down into the chest, around a blood vessel then back up the neck to the larynx, and because of this there are plenty of opportunities for it to become damaged. The test for this condition is to put a camera up the horse's nose and down the back of its throat so that you can see the larynx open and close as the horse breathes.

The clinician in charge, Tom, was a hugely clever, very intense and focused vet, not given to being chatty or wasting time. 'Right, Jo, you're doing this,' he said.

I'd seen it done several times, of course, but watching someone put an endoscope costing thousands of pounds up the nose of a horse that is tossing its head around, especially given that said nose is full of fine blood vessels that can be easily punctured and will then bleed copiously, is very different to doing it yourself. And to make matters worse, the TV crew were there, taking a lot of interest in this case. So, with a camera focused on my face, I gritted my teeth. 'Come on, Mackenzie,' I muttered, 'we're going to do this'. I grabbed his nose, stuck my left forefinger and thumb into his nostrils and pushed the endoscope in under my finger, so that it ran along the bottom, next to the septum. And to my amazement it worked. I turned around to grin at Amy, who was holding the sound boom. She gave me a thumbs-up with her spare hand. I was so pleased that my brief moment of success had been caught on camera.

The endoscope camera confirmed what we suspected; Mackenzie had RLN and would need what's known as a tie-back surgery. I scrubbed in and Tom opened up the side of the neck so that he could reach the larynx. My job was to hold the incision open with retractors, which I did for two hours, with Tom barking 'Open it up more' every few minutes as he stitched open the part of the larynx that kept flopping shut. It was an impressive job, and would mean that Mackenzie could breathe in a significantly larger volume of oxygen and so perform far better. For the next few days I watched Mackenzie closely, doing all his checks and going in regularly to give him a stroke and a few words of encouragement. His progress was excellent; he would be going home before the end of the week and would be back eventing in just a few months' time.

We were all a little in awe of Tom, who had achieved, in addition to his basic veterinary qualifications, a PhD and then a residency at Cornell University, which meant he was both a European and an American specialist in equine surgery, all at a ridiculously young age. Tom loved technology; he always had the latest gadgets, and when he wanted to show us something he would send us a QR code to our phones, rather than an email link. All of which meant that when, towards the end of the week, he handed Lucy his brand new iPad to take some pictures of the colic surgery he was doing, she took hold of it with extreme care. Not quite extreme enough, though, because she didn't realise that the iPad cover was only attached to the iPad by a magnet and as she lifted it for a picture, holding it by the cover, the iPad fell out and smashed on the floor. We all stared at it, speechless with horror.

Tom was aghast, but he had his hands inside the horse,

so there wasn't much he could do except fume, while Lucy turned pale and ran out of the surgical suite.

After that it was hard to concentrate on the colic surgery, which I absolutely needed to do, since I'd scrubbed in and had one arm inside the horse feeling around for its intestines, which Tom was in the process of untwisting. I had no idea what to say, so for the rest of the surgery I kept quiet, tried not to catch Tom's eye and just followed directions when asked to pass a surgical instrument or hold something.

After the operation was over Lucy and I went for a quick cup of tea in the student tea room. 'There's something about horses,' she groaned. 'I just seem to have bad luck when I'm on horse rotations. That would never have happened if it had been a cow.'

I wasn't too sure about the logic of this, but it was one of those times when the only thing to do was to nod sympathetically and pass her a very large slice of cake.

'It's so typical it would happen with Tom,' she groaned, biting into the cake. 'He's the one clinician you really want to impress. What do you think I should do? I mean, he can't honestly expect me to pay for it, can he? I've got a £35,000 student loan to pay off already. I just don't have that sort of cash.'

'Don't worry. I don't think he will expect that. Just get him something to say sorry. I mean, he was the one that asked you take the photos. He took the risk with your butter fingers.'

'Too soon for jokes, Jo,' Lucy replied, although there was the flicker of a smile on her face.

The next day she brought in a bottle of wine with a picture of a sheep on it, and a card saying 'I'm feeling sheepish' on the front, which made Tom smile. He forgave her, and even gave her a good grade for the rotation.

CHAPTER ELEVEN

The Kitten who Thought She Was a Parrot

By late November I had reached a real low. We were in the middle of our two weeks in small animal medicine and it was, to put it mildly, challenging.

To be honest I had dreaded this placement, and it was turning out to be even worse than I had feared.

The problem with this rotation wasn't the patients, which were mostly cuddly and uncomplaining, it was the non-stop pressure of hectic twelve- to fifteen-hour days on which I arrived at and left the almost windowless confines of the Queen Mother Hospital without ever seeing daylight.

I'm a very outdoorsy person. I need to ride, jog, walk or just get outside, or I start to get cabin fever. But on the treadmill that was small animal medicine there was no time even to stick your head out of the door and check that daylight still existed. Breaks were snatched and barely lasted long enough to grab a cup of tea or a biscuit. And inevitably tiredness set in, tempers frayed and grumbling became the order of the day.

Lucy, Grace, Jade, Katy and I were on this rotation with our sister group. So there were ten of us students, each being assigned multiple cases for which we were expected to take charge, and the strain set in pretty much straight away. Even cheerful Charlie looked a bit white-faced by the end of each long, long day.

Each morning I woke at 5.30am to a freezing cold house, threw on my clothes, gulped down half a bowl of cereal and huddled into my coat before venturing out into the cold and dark to de-ice my car.

I had to get to the hospital by 6.30am to start animal checks. On day one we were each assigned multiple cases and from then on we took charge of them. As new animals were admitted to the QMH we were allocated their cases, which happened as frequently or sometimes more frequently than our current cases being discharged or transferred to other departments. So we continually had at least three or four cases on the go, and that meant morning SOAP checks on all of them. In addition to checking their medical state, we also had to clean out kennels and cat cages and take any dogs that were in our care outside so that they could go to the toilet on the square of grass reserved for this purpose. Everyone was supposed to pick up after the dogs, but a lot of them had diarrhoea, so we'd be out there in our dolly shoes tip-toeing through a minefield of dog mess and mud in the dark, thinking 'Please go quickly so we can go back inside' while the dog whose lead you were holding would be sniffing around, taking its time and enjoying the aroma. At least the cats had litter trays.

At around 8am we'd go to the tea room for a welcome cup of tea and to be allocated the new cases that were to come in that day. Each one would have an entry on a consult list for the day that would have the animal's name, breed and a one-line summary of its condition. We'd all fight for the easy cases, which basically meant conditions we understood or ones that looked a little bit more straight-forward. That didn't mean we got them, though! It was a first-come, first-serve situation and we were all ruthless, snatching cases from under each other's noses and ticking them off the list.

Once all our animals were sorted out and assessed, we met the clinicians and had to explain to them what was happening with each animal and what the plan was for its care. And, of course, the clinicians did not accept any plan without asking a dozen challenging questions that made you doubt whether you'd made the right diagnosis after all.

My first case was a kitten called Twinkle. I'd cheated a bit, because my housemate Andrew had been on small animal medicine the week before I started, so I asked him if there were any nice cases he'd worked on that I could take over. He told me Twinkle was cute, so when her case came up I volunteered. But what he hadn't told me was that Twinkle seemed to think she was a parrot.

I laughed when someone first said this, but it was true! Twinkle was a beautiful little blue kitten and her condition had initially been a bit of a mystery. She needed regular examinations, but as soon as you picked her up to have a look at her she would clamber onto your shoulder. And if you tried to stop her, she would just scramble and scratch your neck until she got her way. It was funny, but very frustrating, too. In the end, every time I needed to check her over I had to ask Lucy to come and help so that she could sit on Lucy's shoulder and I could check her there.

Twinkle had come to the hospital a few days earlier because she kept dribbling and pressing her head against the wall at home. Excessive salivating is an indication of nausea, and judging by Twinkle's lack of appetite she certainly wasn't feeling her best.

Based on all of this, and coupled with the fact that she was very young, there was a presumptive diagnosis that Twinkle had a liver shunt caused by an abnormality that had occurred when she was developing in the womb, which meant that blood was bypassing her liver rather than going through it. This had led to a build-up of ammonia in her blood. The liver filters ammonia and converts it to urea, which isn't toxic, but if the blood isn't going through the liver or the liver isn't working, then ammonia builds up. Excess ammonia can lead to many problems, including nausea, but the worst of all is the effect it has on the brain, causing the compulsive head pressing and progressing to seizures, coma and death if left untreated. The condition is otherwise known as hepatic encephalopathy. Twinkle was on lactulose, which takes the strain off the liver by decreasing the uptake of ammonia from the guts, and it seemed to be working quite well. She also was on antibiotics to alter the good bacteria in her gut and stop them producing so much ammonia from the protein in her diet. The alternative would be surgery on her liver, but we hoped she wouldn't need that as she was simply too small for such a major operation at this stage.

My next patient was Bella, an eight-month-old yellow Labrador puppy with chronic, profuse diarrhoea. She was severely dehydrated, so she needed to be on a drip. It isn't easy having a young dog on a drip, because they want to bounce around and tend to get tangled in the tubing, but Bella was feeling rough and she was flopped in the bottom of her kennel, her nose resting on her paws, her big eyes following every move I made.

Despite her tender age, Bella had been in the hospital before. Like Twinkle, she'd had a liver shunt, and at just a few months old she'd had surgery for it. Her recovery had been good, and the condition she'd arrived with on this occasion was unconnected. It was just rotten luck that she'd become sick again.

This time the diarrhoea had not responded to initial treatments by her local vet, so she'd come to us for further investigations, and on my second day in the unit a faecal culture revealed she had Giardia, a protozoan parasite that manifests itself in the gut. This caused a bit of concern, as Giardia can be transmitted to humans, giving them symptoms similar to a severe form of food poisoning.

Until then I'd been enjoying giving Bella lots of cuddles, but the presence of Giardia meant that we had to barrier nurse her, kitting up from head to toe in protective clothing and wearing rubber gloves, and then wash very thoroughly after each examination. I was a bit worried that I might have caught it already, but there wasn't much I could do except wait it out.

Meanwhile, in came Toby, another Labrador puppy, an adorable little chocolate-coloured fellow, just three months old and full of bounce. He had severe diarrhoea, too, so, until we had his tests back, we also had to barrier nurse him. Unlike Bella, Toby was not feeling too bad, and he wanted to play. Like most young dogs he wanted to bite and chew absolutely everything, so despite my protective clothing I was covered with tiny puncture wounds. He would regularly shred my rubber gloves when I was examining him – I got through a couple of pairs each time.

Tests confirmed that Toby also had Giardia, so he was put on the same strong antibiotics as Bella. Both of them needed to stay for a few days so that we could be sure they were on the mend and fully rehydrated.

We students were expected to do absolutely everything for the animals whose cases we were allocated, including taking blood for tests, doing physical checks, giving them their drugs and phoning their owners or seeing them when they came in, as they had to be kept informed. And of course we had to regularly report every single thing back to the clinician in charge.

All three of my patients needed to be checked every couple of hours, so most of my day was spent taking the protective clothing on and off, yelling for Lucy to help me check on Twinkle, trying to avoid Toby's nips, and clearing up after Bella and Toby, a chore that I shared with the veterinary nurses and any other students who happened to be in the vicinity. Neither puppy was able to control their bowels, so there was a lot of clearing up to do.

As Bella began to recover she started chewing through her drip tube, at least four times a day. I put a buster collar on her, one of those funnel-shaped plastic contraptions designed to stop a dog chewing at itself or anything else. She chewed through it. She also developed the habit of peeing on my feet. And when, with the agreement of my supervising clinician, I finally discharged her a few days later, she thanked me by flooding the consulting room floor with a final pee that looked as though she'd been holding it all in for about twenty-four hours.

Next up was a cat called Buttons, a docile tabby with high blood pressure and no appetite. She had to be fed through an oesophageal tube, which took ages as she could only take in two millilitres of liquid food a minute and she had to have fifty-four millilitres per feed – that meant twenty-seven minutes was needed for every feed, several times a day.

I felt as if I were on a merry-go-round of taking barrier clothing on and off to check Toby, feeding Buttons and then going through the whole parrot routine with Twinkle. By the time I'd seen to all of them it was time to start the whole routine again.

To add to our woes, we had to use a totally baffling computer system to record all our patients' results. It was called CRIS and initially we found the name amusing because people would say 'I hate CRIS' or 'I've got CRIS to do,' but that very quickly got boring and the system was still just as confusing.

At the end of each day, as in many of the other rotations, we had rounds with the clinicians in which we'd sit around a table and work through cases as a group. And, true to form, the clinicians had a tendency to put one of us on the spot to see how much we really knew. The fear of being singled out kept us on edge for the whole hour of rounds. It's not easy being singled out, as I'd already discovered in the anaesthesia rotation, and by that time in the day we were so tired it was impossible to think straight.

One evening, the ten of us gathered round the table in the teaching room. The clinician in charge had written 'Hypercalcaemia' on the board, which basically means increased calcium levels in the blood. They started with one person and worked around the group, asking each of us to give a reason why an animal might develop this condition. By the end we'd managed to come up with ten different reasons. Cue a sigh of relief all round, but no, the clinician wanted to go round again – twice. That meant coming up with thirty different potential causes for one condition. Towards the end we really struggled, but the clinician pushed us. They were never nasty, just very, very persistent and in absolutely no hurry to let us go until we'd come up with what they wanted.

Lucy and I did our best to help one another. We had a fair number of muttered confabs in the corridors about how to handle our cases and how to survive the endless days, and we did plenty of grumbling over tepid cups of tea that we never had time to finish. We couldn't imagine how the resident vets stood the long hours and lack of daylight. Some of them were there until eleven at night and back in again at six the next morning. It wasn't a question of short-age of staff – there were plenty of vets and plenty of nurses.

It was about dedication. This was a specialist unit in a specialist hospital and the vets stayed with their cases all the way through. I really admired their commitment.

Our days were supposed to end at 6.30pm, but every couple of days we had to do evening checks, which meant that we didn't finish until nine. When that happened I would get home at 9.30pm, eat anything I could lay my hands on that didn't need cooking and fall into bed, utterly wiped out.

At the end of my first week I went back to Kent for a much-needed weekend with my family and friends. It was a chance for a long-overdue get-together with Abi. We went riding together and it felt like old times, chatting and laughing as we cantered over the fields.

That evening we went out for drinks with a couple of friends and I poured out my woes. It felt good to have a break from the cameras, the clinicians and the endless (diarrhoea-filled) corridors of the QMH.

I started the second week feeling a bit better and I took on the case of Biscuit, a Yorkie that had come in a couple of weeks earlier with tracheal collapse, which is when the cartilage rings holding open the windpipe are weak and can't hold their shape when air passes by. The signs include an awful honking cough, being too weak to exercise and shortness of breath. It's a congenital condition common in small-breed dogs, particularly Yorkshire terriers.

Biscuit was a sweetie, a little black and brown dog with a round face, and he looked just like a teddy bear. When I met his very chatty and friendly owner for the consultation we sat and swapped stories about Yorkies and how lovely they are. This was a follow-up consultation to see how Biscuit was doing, and how he had responded to treatment and advice. He had been given cough suppressants and anti-inflammatories for his airways, but the most vital thing of all was to get him to lose some weight, because as he hadn't been able to exercise he'd got rather chunky. He was a real success story, already looking much slimmer, much stronger and barely coughing. His delighted owner said he was almost back to his old self.

Halfway through the last week I had a brief reprieve. David Bolt, my research supervisor, asked me if I wanted to go with him to a local zoo to rasp donkeys' teeth. He'd been asked to do it by a friend there. I know I've had more bizarre offers, I just can't remember when, but I leaped at the chance of a break and off we went. I was allowed the time off, providing I got friends to cover my cases, so Lucy volunteered to do it in exchange for me covering Wednesday afternoon for her, so that she could slip away for a tennis match.

David told me he hadn't rasped donkeys' teeth for years, which made us about the same standard and we had a lot of fun. Rasping the teeth of donkeys involves holding their surprisingly small mouths open with something called a Hausmann gag and then filing the teeth with a large rasp. Unfortunately when I was mid-rasp the gag slipped and the donkey's teeth clamped shut on my hand. I yelped. It felt as though my whole hand had been crushed and I was convinced it was broken. I hate making a fuss so I gritted my teeth and carried on, although much more slowly, while constantly checking that the gag wasn't slipping again. The next day my whole hand was black and blue, and there was a large swelling on the back of it, but at least I could still move it. Despite this I really enjoyed my day out; it was a nice change and it felt wonderful to be outdoors for a few hours.

Back at the QMH, over the next few days I had a couple of very sad cases. The first was Riley, a sweet-tempered, chunky old golden retriever of about ten or eleven, grey around the muzzle and slowing down. He came in with yellow gums and eyes. He was severely jaundiced and clearly felt awful. So much so that he didn't need any sedation for an ultrasound or a needle biopsy of his liver. He just lay quietly and let us get on with the tests.

It was clear that Riley was very ill, and I knew that his was not going to be a case with a happy outcome, so to stop myself from breaking down I tried to stay upbeat. I was being filmed at this point and one of the cameramen, a new member of the crew, took me aside to say that my cheery attitude might come across badly to the general public, since Riley was very ill.

I felt ridiculously upset. He wasn't being unkind, just pointing out a bit of an incongruity, but I was finding the whole week hard, I was tired and, of course, I always worried about how I'd come across on camera anyway. The thought of millions of people watching me felt quite over-whelming at times.

I struggled on, as the crew followed me while I gently led Riley from the ultrasound suite back to the ward. Just outside the doors of the ward Riley produced a profuse amount of diarrhoea all over the corridor, which I had to clean up. As I mopped, Riley stood next to me and produced more. This happened over and over again. Poor Riley just couldn't help it, but trying to clear it all up was a nightmare, and through it all the film crew just kept filming. I felt hopeless and tired and annoyed, and I just wanted them to stop. That evening I went home and cried. The whole fortnight had been hard, and Riley's case was the hardest of all.

The next day his biopsy results came back, and they weren't good. He had a large tumour infiltrating his liver. Despite a poor prognosis, his owners wanted to give him every chance, so he was transferred to the oncology depart-ment to start chemotherapy. This might at least allow him an extra few months with his owners, but we all knew that he probably didn't have long to live and the atmosphere in the department was subdued.

Next up was Oscar, a seven-year-old collie-greyhound crossbreed. He was huge, not far off the size of a wolf-hound, grey and white, with a face like an Old English sheepdog. Poor Oscar had been having sneezing fits for months. This could have been due to something benign and fixable, like a grass seed that had got stuck up his nose, or something life-threatening like a tumour. It was a very uncertain time for his worried owners as there was no way to tell how serious it was until we investigated.

The choice we had was either to put a camera up his nose or to take a CT scan. You can see more with a CT scan as it's three-dimensional, but to be sure, in the end we opted for both. While he was under the anaesthetic we did a rhinoscopy (camera up his nose), but we couldn't find anything. However, the CT scan revealed a tumour at the top of his nose that had worked its way through the bone between his brain and his nostrils. It had penetrated his brain, which meant there was nothing we could do.

In the few days that he was with us I had a lot of cuddles with Oscar and I spent a lot of time with him. Once the diagnosis was made, his heartbroken owners were informed and he went home to spend some time with them. When they were ready, and when they felt that Oscar no longer had quality of life, they would bring him back for the final time and we would put him to sleep.

By now we needed a bit of light relief, and Charlie provided it. He had decided to grow a moustache for Movember – an annual event held to raise money for prostate cancer – and by our second week it had sprouted fulsomely and was a truly hideous handlebar affair that Charlie twirled with gruesome pleasure. However, the producers of *Young Vets* were not happy; they needed continuity in the films and they certainly didn't want Charlie suddenly appearing with a horrendous moustache. There was an impasse; despite their pleas Charlie refused to remove it and in the end they had no choice but to film him with it.

He did shave it off a few days early, though. He and I were due to do what they called a 'master interview' along with Grace. The idea was to sit around talking about being vets, sharing experiences and funny short anecdotes, and the producer, Isobel, put her foot down. The moustache had to go. She gave Charlie a £50 donation to the Movember charity and his pride was satisfied. The moustache went.

When he eventually saw himself in the programme, as we all watched a preview, he blushed crimson at the point when the moustache made its unexplained appearance.

'Why didn't they say something to explain it,' he spluttered. 'I thought they'd say what it was about.' We had no sympathy, Charlie became the clown of the show and his moustache caused endless hilarity. 'At least you didn't have it for the master interview,' Grace teased him. 'It could have been so, so much worse.'

The other highlight of the second week was Thanksgiving, which fell on the day before we finished the rotation. It had become a tradition in our house, with two American students living there, for all five of us to get together for a Thanksgiving dinner. The college sold its own home-reared and humanely slaughtered turkeys and we pooled our resources to buy one, which John then cooked with the full trimmings, including pumpkin pie for dessert. It was a feast we all looked forward to every year, and Kevin and James travelled back for it from the far-flung locations where they were involved with, respectively, sheep and zoo animals.

By our final day I couldn't wait to finish this rotation. I just wanted to pass and go home for a quiet weekend to catch up on sleep. We were graded in three areas at the end of each rotation: professionalism, knowledge and application of skills. On the last day we had a one-to-one feedback session, which the film crew decided it would be fun to include. I was dreading being given poor results on camera, but to my immense surprise I was awarded pass, pass and distinction. I came out of the room, to where Charlie was waiting his turn to get feedback and gave him a high-five.

The cameras left me and joined him for his moment in the hot seat, and all I could think as I walked down the corridor towards the exit was, wow, how on earth did that happen?

CHAPTER TWELVE

Mad Cows and Doris the Goat

It was the middle of December, early on a freezing cold, foggy day and the last thing I needed was a face-off with some very grumpy cows. One of them looked as though it was about to head-butt me and a couple of others were straining against the decidedly flimsy-looking gate that separated them from the yard where I was standing.

I looked round for Niall, the vet I was assisting, and the farmer who owned the cows. He'd asked us to come and test the whole herd for pregnancy, which would mean getting up close and personal with every single one of them.

'They look a bit excitable.' I tried not to sound worried.

'They're not used to being handled,' the farmer said cheerfully. 'Beef heifers, you see, not dairy cows these. So they get a bit frisky.'

I could see that. They looked like a bunch of over-excited children, pushing and shoving to get to the back of a queue for matron. Only these particular 'children' weighed around half a tonne each – and that could present a very real danger.

Niall had already warned me about the difficulties of working with cattle. A few years earlier he had been kicked by a cow, fallen over and been trampled by two others before the farmer could rescue him. It had taken him six months to recover.

'Stay well clear,' he said, 'keep your eyes on them and be ready to move fast. Oh, and make sure you have insurance.'

Right. Bit late for that now.

I eyed the cows. I'd met some very cooperative heifers during the previous few months of my training and I was feeling pretty confident about pregnancy testing, but this lot were clearly in the mood for a fight and I didn't fancy our chances.

Niall was a slightly eccentric Irishman with a skip to his voice and a full head of white hair, which he insisted had turned at an abnormally early age. He was the senior vet and the owner of a medium-sized mixed practice in East Sussex, where I was doing another two weeks' work experience. Alongside Niall there were eight other vets and twelve nursing and support staff. The practice was based in a semi-rural area, so it covered small animals, farm animals like cows, pigs and goats, horses, alpacas (there were a couple of herds locally) and even deer. This meant that working there gave me a fantastic opportunity to try a bit of everything – including handling stroppy cows.

'Let's get them into the yard,' Niall said, 'and then we can pen them one by one.'

Niall and I, both dressed in wellies and waterproof trousers and jackets, joined the farmer in shooing the cows through a metal barred gate into the small muddy yard beyond. From here we would lead them one at a time into the pen where, once inside, it would be impossible for them to turn around and we could approach them from behind more easily.

As usual, the plan was for one of us to plunge an arm into the cow and feel for a foetus and then confirm the diagnosis with a scanner, inserted rectally. The art of diagnosing pregnancy manually is gradually becoming obsolete, giving way to diagnosing with a scanner, but whenever I shadowed vets for work experience they always made an effort to do both so that I would learn. Diagnosing manually is easy if the cow is more than a few months pregnant, and is the best way to diagnose how far along the pregnancy is if it is more than three months. However, a scanner picks up much earlier pregnancies, which are hard to feel, as well as checking the status of the ovaries if the cow is not pregnant. So there are pros and cons to both.

With the first cow in the pen, Niall approached, sleeves rolled up, plastic glove on and fingers flexing. But when the cow realised something unfamiliar was going on at her rear end she began to kick and struggle. Niall had to get right into the pen with her, avoid her back hooves and get his arm inside her thrashing behind. At that moment I wouldn't have swapped places with him for a free pass through my exams.

'Right,' he said, after cow number five. 'Fancy a go?'

My heart started racing. I'm always up for a challenge – I tend to bowl in and have a go at anything, however scary. But at that moment what I fancied, as a particularly cantankerous cow thrust past and almost knocked me flying, was a hot shower, some dry clothes and a cup of tea.

'OK,' I said, sounding what I hoped was upbeat and enthusiastic.

'You can get in with this one then,' Niall grinned, pointing at the cow being thrust into the pen. 'She looks quieter than the others.'

'Really?' She didn't look quieter to me. In fact she looked particularly demented, with eyes wild and nostrils flaring, a bit like the Hannibal Lecter of the cow world.

'Yes, she's a good girl this,' the farmer added.

'Fine, great, no problem,' I muttered, pulling on the plastic glove that reached to my elbow and approaching the pen.

It didn't help that the film crew were there, although by that time I was very fond of Amy and Rob. We'd spent so much time together and they'd seen me through so many scrapes that we'd become good friends. But while I enjoyed their company, I was still aware that they were recording my every mishap for posterity.

That day they'd brought along a new cameraman, Ash, who seemed just as friendly and easygoing as they were. The three of them had decided to begin the day's filming by recording my journey to work, so they'd arrived at the house at the crack of dawn that morning to find Dad wandering out of the shower wearing a towel and Mum on a bed on the floor downstairs where she'd been sleeping with Tosca to stop her waking everyone up at three in the morning.

Tosca was doing well. In fact the indications were that the brain tumour might have slowed down its growth, but that didn't stop her from becoming more annoying in her old age. Because she was completely blind she had no idea when dawn was, so whenever she woke up she insisted everyone else should wake up, too. If nobody woke up to keep her company she would whine and pace the house, bumping into everything and knocking things over. So Mum had started taking her downstairs when she woke up and going back to sleep down there with her, to stop her from waking everyone else.

Mum and Dad were both a little embarrassed, so I gulped down the last of my tea, swallowed my toast and shoved Amy, Rob and Ash out of the door. They decided to film me driving off and made me do it twice, because the first take wasn't right, which was a little frustrating as we were already running late. When I finally got going Ash went with me in the car to film my journey from inside, but as I'd run out of screen-wash the windscreen was a grimy mess and he had to try to film the road ahead of us between the smears.

All this before eight on a dark winter morning, and now here I was, facing the rear end of a stroppy cow with the three of them there to record it. I took a deep breath and slipped in through the gate, hoping the cow wouldn't notice.

She did. It was like trying to examine a super-charged bucking bronco. I had one arm inside her, the other holding onto her tail and my feet as far back as I could get them in an attempt to avoid her thrashing hooves. I must have looked pretty demented myself. And then suddenly …

'I can feel it, she's pregnant, there's a calf here and it's pretty far on, I'd say about six, maybe seven months,' I yelled. No matter how many times I did this, it was still absolutely amazing to feel the growing calf, curled up inside its mother.

Niall smiled. 'Put that one down as heavy in calf then, and let's get the next one in.'

I backed out of the gate and peeled off the glove, a wide grin on my face. Having felt the developing calf, knowing there was a healthy young animal that would soon be born, was a reminder of why, despite the long hours, the cold, the mud and the stroppy cows, I wanted to be a vet. I couldn't imagine any other job like it.

But there was a tough side to what we were doing, too. Some of the cows that were pregnant were too young to have calves and we had to inject them with a compound called prostaglandin, to induce terminations. A ten-month-old heifer is too small to manage a natural birth, so she will either die in the process or, if she's lucky and the vet gets there in time, have a caesarean. Apart from the danger to her of such a complex birth, the cost to the farmer of the caesarean is often more than the heifer is worth, so it's a bad idea in both health and economic terms.

Niall gave me the job of injecting the young pregnant heifers with prostaglandin, which was a little easier than getting in behind them. For most I was able to inject them through the bars of the holding pen.

Most of the cows we checked had put up a fight, although we eventually managed to work our way through them reasonably safely. All bar one. Realising that her friends were now in the field and she was the only one left in the pen, the last cow panicked and attempted to jump the metal gate. She hurled herself at it right beside Amy, Rob and Ash, who got a massive shock, abandoned the segment they were filming and ran across the yard.

It made for a hilarious blooper, but what wasn't hilarious was that we now had to go and round up this wild-eyed cow and get her back into the pen away from her friends. It took us all of half an hour before she was in the pen again and we were able to finish our job.

By the time we'd finished checking all twenty-eight cows, seventeen of which were pregnant, we were filthy and exhausted. After a hose-down in the farmyard we stripped off our waterproofs, bundled them into the back of Niall's car and headed back to the surgery, where I rushed to check on Nipper, a little Jack Russell recovering in the kennels after an operation to remove a thorn that had worked its way into his paw. He was awake but still a bit sleepy, his tail wagging and already up on his bandaged paw. I gave him a cuddle. 'You'll be going home this afternoon, Nipper.' True to his name, he gave me a playful nip as I tried to whip my hand away. 'Ouch, you need to learn some manners,' I said, rubbing the place where his sharp little teeth had grazed me.

'Grab some lunch,' Niall called. 'Half an hour, then we'll get out on rounds.'

We'd been on the go since eight that morning and I knew the rounds would probably take us till past six. I'd been hoping to get home in time to ride Elli and Tammy, neither of whom was showing signs of getting any thinner. But by the time I drove home it would be past seven and too late. One thing I had learned on rotations was that being a vet meant very long days as well as tough, physical work. Even in a placement like this, a ten- or twelve-hour day was normal.

By one o'clock I felt hungry enough to eat one of the cows we'd just been to visit, so I was grateful for the chance to sit down and enjoy my longed-for cheese sandwich. But as I opened my mouth for the first bite Susie the receptionist stuck her head round the door.

'We've got Mrs Brown in the car park. She's worried about Doris. Niall says can you pop out and see her? He will be out to join you soon.'

I gazed longingly at my slab of crusty bread and cheese, stuffed it back into my bag and headed out to the car park, where a very stylish black SUV was parked.

Out climbed a smartly dressed woman.

'Hello, Mrs Brown. My name's Jo. I'm a final-year vet student. Niall is just on his way, but has sent me out to get started. How can I help?'

'I'm concerned about Doris. She's just not herself at the moment and I'm not sure what's wrong. I've been giving her special food and lots of attention but she's being a bit listless and quiet, and it's not like her normal behaviour at all.'

'OK, let's have a look and try to find out what the problem is while we wait for Niall,' I said, in what I hoped was a reassuring and professional way. 'Is Doris in the back?'

Mrs Brown said she was and went to open the boot. I expected to find a cat or perhaps a small dog curled up in a basket. So it was a bit of a surprise to find a very large, handsome white goat sitting in the back of the car regarding me with what appeared to be extreme boredom.

'Oh,' I said. 'She's a goat.'

Mrs Brown looked at me as though I was a little odd. 'Of course she's a goat. What did you expect?'

Anything but a goat, I thought, smiling brightly at her.

'So Doris is feeling unwell, is she?'

'Well, maybe unwell, I don't know. She gets the very best of everything, but I can tell she's not her usual self.'

'Would you like to get her out of the car and I'll give her an examination?' I suggested.

'I'm afraid Doris doesn't like getting out of the car. She gets upset. She only gets out when we're at home. Can you look at her here?'

'Yes, er, of course,' I said, still smiling with a grin that was beginning to feel a bit rictus-like. And so I climbed into the back of the SUV, checked Doris's temperature and heart rate and gave her a good nose-to-tail check – or as good a one as I could manage with her lying down on her cosy blanket in the back of the car and me squashed in beside her.

Her vital signs were all fine, but her stomach was large. 'I wonder if she could be pregnant,' I said.

Mrs Brown's face lit up. 'Oh, do you think she could be?' she asked. 'It would make sense. I have a couple of billies as well as my three nannies. Maybe one could have got to her without me knowing. I'd be so happy, another little kid to add to our family, and more wonderful milk from Doris – I sell it you know, it's so much healthier than cow's milk, and it makes the most wonderful yoghurt and cream.'

She was still extolling the virtues of goat's milk five minutes later. I interrupted, as politely as I could. 'It sounds like marvellous stuff. Let me go and talk to Niall, and we'll see if we can scan Doris and let you know for sure.'

I headed back inside and explained the situation. 'Oh yes, Doris,' Niall said. 'She's a very spoilt goat. She absolutely refuses to get out of the car. Tell Mrs Brown to back up to the large animal unit round the side and we'll bring out the ultrasound scanner.'

And so as Doris reclined regally in the car, I crouched next to her in the back, holding her still, while Niall brought out the scanner and Mrs Brown stood by, hopping from foot to foot.

'Oh, dear Doris, she will need all kinds of special foods if she's expecting,' she exclaimed.

Niall studied the scanner and then turned to her. 'One large, healthy kid on the way,' he said. 'Congratulations, Doris. And Mrs Brown.'

As I unfurled myself from the back of the car and staggered into the surgery, still bent double and desperate to retrieve my sandwich, Mrs Brown tucked Doris in, closed the boot and drove merrily on her way.

'You ready yet?' Niall called. 'We need to get going. We've got an alpaca, several pigs, a horse and another goat to see.'

I gulped the last crust of my sandwich and leaped to my feet.

'Coming.'

We spent the afternoon looking at some calves that had pneumonia and a sheep whose head was tilting to one side. It had also lost its sight. Niall thought it had cerebrocortical necrosis (CCN), which is a common neurological disease that comes from a deficiency of thiamine, a type of vitamin B. I wasn't so sure, though. I remembered that CCN doesn't usually include head tilt, but rather the sheep look up (it's called 'star-gazing'), and I suspected that this sheep might have listeria instead, a bacterial infection, which would mean it needed antibiotics, not vitamins. After a couple of days, when it hadn't improved with vitamin treatment, it was put on antibiotics, which led to an immediate improvement.

I had been right, which was a small victory that I kept to myself but cherished, since in between calls Niall enjoyed quizzing me relentlessly on every aspect of treatment and pointing out with some relish anything I got wrong.

At the end of the day our last call was to revisit an alpaca. There were several herds of these woolly South American camelids in the area. They look a bit like small llamas, or sheep with very long necks. They produce gorgeous wool, soft, warm and much prized, and generally they adapt well to life in Britain. But this particular alpaca, a very pretty, creamy-coated chap, was lying on the ground, his hind limbs paralysed after some kind of trauma to the spine. We'd seen him earlier in the afternoon and Niall had told the owner that there was nothing we could do – the only option was humane euthanasia.

The owner had said she wanted to talk to her husband first and, as the alpaca wasn't in pain, we had agreed to come back. Now it was late afternoon and the owner had gone out, preferring not to be around for the procedure, after giving us permission to put the alpaca gently to sleep.

I never like euthanasia calls, although there is something comforting about the fact that vets can end an animal's pain and suffering. I had made a deal with myself that once I graduated I would always try to put myself in the animal's position before making choices about death, and if there was a chance that the animal could get better I would fight for it. But if it was likely to continue to suffer or was simply being kept alive for the owner's sake I would put it out of its misery.

As we pulled up at the end of the driveway, the house and the grounds were eerily quiet.

Although the owner hadn't wanted to be present for the euthanasia, Niall wanted to make sure no one was at home who might like to attend, so he made his way to the house to check while I put my farm gear on beside the car.

At college we'd been taught the best way to get ready for farm visits was by rolling our waterproof trousers over our wellingtons before we put them on, so that we could simply step into the boots and pull up the trousers; a fantastic tip for those like me who are so uncoordinated that the visit would be over by the time we were ready.

I was just pulling up my waterproofs when a piercing screech resonated from the house.

'Well, they're not in,' Niall yelled, over what must have been the loudest burglar alarm I had ever heard.

'How did you manage to set that off?' I said.

'There was no answer when I was banging on the doors and then I noticed a window was slightly open, so I leaned in and called out to see if anyone was home and it set the damn thing off.'

Knowing Niall, who I was beginning to realise could be really quite eccentric, I wouldn't have been surprised if he'd climbed in, but I kept that thought to myself.

With the alarm still screeching in the background – I'm sure people could hear it for a radius of several miles – we headed out to the field where the alpaca was. As I stroked his woolly head and murmured comforting words to him,

Niall administered the anaesthetic overdose and the alpaca closed his eyes for the last time.

The owners had asked for a partial post-mortem for insurance purposes and we needed to do it immediately because the alpaca was too large to take away with us.

'I don't think it's fair to do it in front of the other alpacas,' I said. There were about ten of them lined up along the fence, peering across at us.

'Quite right,' Niall agreed. 'Let's take that wheelbarrow over there and we can move him away from the field to some flat ground.'

Which was how, a few minutes later, the two of us came to be wheeling a dead alpaca across a field in a bright orange wheelbarrow when a police car, blue lights flashing, pulled up in front of us.

'Excuse me,' said an officer, climbing out of the car. 'We've had a 999 call reporting a rather strange situation. Could you explain what's going on here?'

Niall looked at me.

'It's never a boring day when you're a vet, Jo.'

That evening I managed a quick ride on Tammy before rushing home to celebrate Dad's birthday with the family. His parents had come over from their home in Crowborough, East Sussex. Grandma and Grandpa Hardy are lovely, always interested in everything that's going on in my life and ready with a thousand questions. We can't see them as often as my other grandparents, Grandma and Grandpa Nevison, who live next door, so when we do it's a real treat.

Grandma and Grandpa Hardy are famous for their Sunday afternoon teas. We used to go over to them when I was little and they would give us the most enormous tea ever, with toast loaded with jam and honey, Scotch pancakes with maple syrup, saffron cake and Grandma's famous trifle, known in the family as the Hardy Substantial. The only savoury thing was Marmite, and we'd each have a piece of toast and Marmite to start with, before overloading on sugar. I used to absolutely love it, but I would eat so much I'd be groaning all the way home.

By the end of the week I was ready for the Christmas holidays. I'd baked muffins to take in, to say thank you to everyone, and towards the end of the afternoon several of the nursing and reception staff began getting into the Christmas spirit, putting on paper hats, swapping cracker presents and reading out cringe-making jokes.

Vicky, one of the vets, came in for a muffin and a cup of tea. 'You lot might be getting excited,' she said, taking a large bite, 'but for us vets Christmas can be hard work. We get inundated with phone calls from people whose dogs have overloaded on chocolate, swallowed cracker toys or eaten turkey bones.'

'Do you often end up having to come in?' I asked.

'Every year,' she said. 'Last year I had to come in on Christmas Day for a spaniel that had eaten a whole box of chocolates. The owner kept saying, "But my aunt always gave her dog chocolate and he lived to fifteen with no problems." And I had to explain that her aunt's dog was exceptionally lucky, because chocolate is toxic for dogs and leads to vomiting and diarrhoea and even seizures. Her spaniel was very unwell and had to be made to throw up with an injection of apomorphine.

'What gets me,' she added, waving the remains of her muffin in the air, 'is that people just don't stop to think that we vets might actually like to have Christmas with our families, instead of rushing to the surgery because they've been thoughtless or careless with their dog.'

Niall came into the room in time to catch the end of this little diatribe. 'Too true,' he said. 'Every vet knows they'll probably spend Christmas dealing with some emergency or other. A couple of years back I had a retriever that had gobbled down the Christmas pudding, and the raisins gave it kidney failure. The poor thing ended up in intensive care. Better make the most of this one, Jo. It might be the last peaceful Christmas you get for a while.'

He downed a gulp of tea. 'Ready to hit the road? We've got to go and see to a goose with a damaged wing.'

I'd been hoping to sneak off early, but no such luck. The goose had not been keen to cooperate and it had taken a near-military operation to pin it down. Two hours later it had its wing strapped and we'd dropped our kit back at the surgery, which by that time was deserted. Longing to get home to a warm fire and supper, I thanked Niall for being a great mentor and reached for my coat. He patted me on the back. 'Lots of luck, Jo,' he said, with a rare smile. As he walked away he called over his shoulder, 'Do you know, Jo, I think you may just have the makings of a decent vet.'

CHAPTER THIRTEEN

'Happy Christmas, Clunky'

Home for Christmas, and I couldn't wait. A whole two weeks off, without having to think about textbooks, diagnoses and beady-eyed clinicians. Time to relax with the family, which meant food, games, walks and riding my horses. And best of all, Jacques was coming over from South Africa to spend the holiday with us.

He was due in a couple of days, but before that the film crew had decided they wanted to come and film me and Ross decorating our Christmas tree. Only one small problem there – we didn't have a tree yet. Ross and I rushed out to get one, but it was the Saturday before Christmas and all the trees had gone except for the ones nobody wanted, with crooked trunks, spindly branches and a bare stalk sticking up at the top. We picked the least sad of the bunch, were still charged an extortionate amount, and loaded it into the back of the car. Once we got it home we spent a hilarious hour trying to get it to stand upright. It had a distinct tilt, so Ross spun it round and propped things under the side of the tree-holder while I stood across the room, hands on hips, saying, 'No, up a bit, down a bit, to the right, round that way,' until he threw a cushion at me and said, 'That's it, I give up.' Tosca was excited by all the commotion and the smell of something different in the house, but moving the furniture to fit in the tree didn't do her any favours. Trying to get to grips with the new layout of the room she ended up knocking the tree so that it tilted again, at which point we realised we were fighting a losing battle trying to keep it upright.

When Amy and Ash arrived they stared at the tree aghast, but there wasn't much choice at that point. Ross and I set to, chattering happily and covering its spindly little branches with shiny baubles as they tried to film us from clever angles to make it look less unfortunate. In the Hardy household we had a wonderful box of Christmas decorations, which, the minute it emerged each year, reduced me and Ross to eight-year-olds again. It was full of red wooden characters and trains, tinsel, beautiful shiny baubles in all sorts of shapes, and a long coil of red fairy lights, half of which now didn't work. We had to try to wind the lights round the tree so that all the broken ones were at the back, a feat that took time and advanced contortion skills.

Once we'd done our best with the tree and had propped a drunken-looking fairy at a precarious angle on the top, Amy and Ash, hoping for something a little more impressive, decided to come with me to see the horses. I was delighted, as it was a chance to show off Tammy and Elli and put them through their paces for the cameras. But predictably, Tammy, who can be a darling or a devil, chose to be the latter. With the camera trained on her she played up in every way she knew, jumping around with her ears back and stubbornly refusing to do anything I asked. Half of the footage involved her prancing on the spot with me saying 'Calm down, calm down' in my most patient voice, despite wanting to bawl at her. The rest of the footage was of us jumping a line of big jumps, mostly at breakneck speed.

Thankfully Elli was far better behaved, but by the time I rode her the light was fading, so although she strutted her stuff, let me ride her bareback and generally showed Tammy how it should be done, the crew said it was probably too dark for the footage to be used. Guess which footage made it into the programme!

After that, Amy and Ash took off, waving goodbye and saying they'd see me in the New Year. I'd got used to having them tailing me and at times it was quite comforting to have a little gang alongside me but, in the nicest possible way, it was good to see the back of them for a couple of weeks.

The following day was Sunday and time for our church nativity play. We're members of our local church; Ross and

I both play in the band, Dad is a church Elder, and Mum is deputy washer of the communion glasses. The family nativity is always a highlight; children and adults all get involved and the traditional story is given a modern twist. This year they were adding in a journalist who would report the story, popping up every now and then with 'Now let's flash forward and see how Mary and Joseph are feeling.'

Dad inevitably plays a shepherd because of the very convincing West Country accent he likes to put on. Embarrassingly, imitating accents is a Hardy male trait, Ross and Dad won't stop once they start, especially when they're together, and between them they can pretty much replicate any accent across the world. Dad's speciality is Cornish and Ross loves to mimic Russian, probably because he plays *Call of Duty* on his Xbox so often, although all he can actually say is 'Cover me, I'm reloading.'

For the nativity Dad had to provide his own costume and he'd left it to the last minute. Searching around for inspiration he picked up the living room sheepskin rug and tied it round himself with some baling twine we had lying around, from the hay bales at the yard. After topping the outfit off with a tea-towel on his head he looked completely ridiculous, strutting around talking like Ted from *The Fast Show*. Ross and I were both cringing, but in the end the nativity was brilliant and Dad had everyone in stitches.

That evening we went out to supper with some family friends at a pub out in the country and there was a tempestuous storm. The rain was so torrential that by the time we set off for home the roads were flooded. Luckily we'd taken our Land Rover Defender or we certainly wouldn't have made it back.

The storm was so severe that large parts of Kent were flooded and dozens of properties damaged after the River Medway burst its banks. We were very lucky that we weren't in a flooded area, but later we learned that four of our livery yard's stables had collapsed, though luckily none of the horses were hurt. The buildings had literally been lifted off their footings, over the heads of their occupants, and blown across the yard owner's garden. Thankfully Tammy and Elli's stables were still standing, although theirs were partially flooded. Tammy was left standing in two inches of water and was pretty unsettled because the horses that lost their stables had escaped and were galloping wildly around.

Jacques was due to arrive at Heathrow early the next morning. I set off in plenty of time, but the traffic was so heavy that I ended up getting there forty-five minutes after his plane had landed. I managed to sprint across the airport to the arrival gate and got there, madly out of breath, just before he appeared. Minutes later I leaped into his arms, thrilled to see him, and he picked me up and spun me around.

'What took you so long? I've been here for ages,' I joked.

'Mmm, sure you have. When are you ever early?' he said, putting me back down on the floor.

'OK, you rumbled me, I've just got here. But pretty good timing all the same, right?'

But Jacques was too distracted for jokes. He had made it to England – but his suitcase hadn't. We spent another hour in the airport while he spoke to various staff and they searched for his case, but it appeared to have vanished and in the end we had to leave without it.

Jacques was wearing a T-shirt and jeans. His coat, along with everything else, was in his luggage. He did have a jumper with him but he insisted that he wasn't worried about the cold – unlike most people who grow up in hot countries, he doesn't seem to feel it. If anything it's the heat he minds.

We went out later that day to get him a change of clothes and a toothbrush. He was still in his T-shirt and I kept telling him to please for goodness sake put on the jumper because it was late December and freezing. But he just didn't seem to feel it.

'I'm really not cold at all,' he insisted, while shoppers in coats and scarves turned to look at him.

'Well, please put a jumper on for me then. You're embarrassing!'

His tolerance of the cold was well and truly tested that afternoon when I took him down to the stables with me to muck out the horses and check on the flooding. He got stuck in without a word of complaint, which earned him a fair few Brownie points.

That evening the staff at Heathrow called to say they had found his case, which probably came in on a later flight, and would send it down to us with a driver that evening. He was relieved to have his clothes but I teased him: 'Never mind your clothes; I'm just glad my Christmas present is here.'

We were all at breakfast the next morning when the phone went. It was a friend of Mum's who worked for a local animal rescue charity. They had a dog, a Staffie, which was in a local pound and was due to be put down that evening. Pounds can only keep dogs for a relatively short time, and if they're not claimed or homed they have to be put to sleep as they just don't have space to keep them. The friend asked Mum whether she would go and pick him up and keep him overnight. A foster home was being arranged, but they wouldn't be able to take him until the next day – Christmas Eve.

Mum asked if we would mind. Of course we all said we'd love to have him and Mum said good, because she'd already agreed. She's a dog-lover, and at the thought of a dog needlessly losing its life, especially at Christmas, she was ready to drop everything and go to its rescue. The pound was a thirty-minute drive away, so, calling out that she would be back in just over an hour, she shot out of the door, still shrugging on her coat.

She arrived back leading a black Staffie with a comical white patch over one eye. His name was Chunky. He was young, perhaps only three or four, and he was almost blind. He charged into the house and banged into everything and everyone, jumping all over the furniture and all of us so that we re-named him Clunky.

The Staffordshire bull terrier is a medium-sized, very popular English breed, squat, muscular and not the prettiest of dogs. A lot of people think they're aggressive and mean – probably because that's how they look – but Staffies are actually much softer in nature than they appear; they can be reliable, intelligent, affectionate and very good with children.

Clunky, however, was not yet ready to be an ambassador for his breed. After half an hour of manically racing round the house knocking everything over, including Tosca, we decided we'd better keep him in the conservatory at the back. Two blind dogs together was just not a good combination. I took him out there with a bowl of food, water and a bed, and spent a bit of time calming him down. Poor Clunky was clearly very unsettled; he'd gone from one place to another and didn't know where he lived or who owned him. Any dog finds this disconcerting, and for a dog that is also blind it's especially hard. Clunky probably hadn't had much human contact in recent weeks and he was desperate for attention.

Throughout the rest of the day all five of us took turns taking him out to the garden and then taking him into the conservatory and doing our best to settle him. But he remained jumpy and edgy, and it was hard work to get him to sleep. Jacques, who has a soft spot for Staffies, spent a lot of time with him and seemed to have a natural touch; he soothed Clunky and eventually got him settled down on his bed.

That night Mum and Dad took Tosca and Paddy upstairs with them, and I decided to sleep downstairs with Clunky. I didn't want to leave him alone all night – he didn't know what to do with himself and might well bark, cry, chew the furniture or hurl himself around. Jacques offered to do it, but I said no, he was still tired from travelling and he needed to sleep. I made up a bed for myself on the living room floor and took Clunky in there with me, putting his bed next to mine.

Despite my ministrations it took him a few hours to settle down, during which he paced restlessly, jumping on me every time I was in danger of falling asleep. Eventually, however, he fell asleep next to me and we all had a few hours of peace.

Mum's friend rang back after breakfast. A foster home had been found for Clunky in Cornwall, and to get him there would involve a relay of drivers. Mum was asked to do the first leg of the journey and take him to the M25, where the next driver would meet her. He would be at his new foster home in time for Christmas Day. From there he would have treatment for his eyes, and some training, before being advertised for adoption into a permanent home. 'Happy Christmas, Clunky,' I said, giving him a last cuddle. 'Don't worry, you'll be all right, there's a good home waiting for you.'

I waved goodbye as his milky eyes peered out of the back of Mum's car, and I felt sad to see him go. We'd bonded during our night on the living room floor and although I was tired, I felt incredibly happy that he was going to have a fresh chance at life. It would be desperately sad to put a young dog like that to sleep, just because no one wanted him. Clunky deserved a loving family and a warm, safe home.

On Christmas Day we had a full house, with both sets of grandparents and plenty of other family and friends. After endless opening of presents and an enormous lunch, rounded off with one of Grandma Hardy's Substantials – a mammoth trifle that would probably feed us all for a month – we set out for a walk. After that, Jacques and I went to the yard to visit the horses and feed them, before collapsing back at home in a warm, over-fed, happy daze.

Whenever Jacques comes to visit, Grandma and Grandpa Hardy like to recall the story of when they were in South Africa and they saw a lion kill a warthog. They always start with, 'When I was in South Africa … have you heard this story?' When we murmur, 'Yes, actually we have,' they carry on with, 'Well, let me tell it to you again …' and off they go. Their trip to South Africa a few years earlier was a present from Dad, my uncle and my twin aunts, and it was such a highlight for them that no one really minds hearing the stories again, even if it is for the umpteenth time.

Jacques and I decided to go up to London after Christmas to visit the Natural History Museum for the Wildlife Photographer of the Year exhibition, and then go on to see *The Lion King*, a musical that's close to both our hearts.

Jacques is a very accomplished wildlife photographer himself, and he loved walking around the exhibition, viewing incredible photos, many by photographers he knew. I told him he should enter some of his own photographs the following year. I was sure his work was good enough.

We managed to get standing tickets for *The Lion King*, after running around Leicester Square ticket offices and the theatre's booking office. I loved it, although Jacques insisted on pointing out the flaws in the animal combinations and the costumes.

That night, after a really happy day together, we got on the train home and I took it as an opportunity to bring up a deeper conversation.

'Soooooo, today has been nice, hasn't it? Are you enjoying your stay in England?' I said.

'Of course, I'm with you. I always enjoy my time with you,' Jacques replied.

'Thank you, I love being with you, too, but what do you think of England? If you take me out of the equation …'

'Why?' he asked. 'It wouldn't be in the equation without you.'

'Yes, but what I'm trying to get at is, do you like it enough to stay here in the long term. Or do you see us in South Africa?'

'Either, love,' he replied. 'But why do you need to talk about that now? That kind of decision is still ages away, and we should cross that bridge when we come to it.'

'Yes, but surely we should at least explore and discuss our options. You could come here and do environmental work, or I could be a vet there. Maybe Thys wants to take on another vet soon so he can slow down and retire?'

'Jo, stop now,' he asserted. 'We will talk about it, but not now. We don't know what our circumstances are going to be in a few years' time, so just drop it, please.'

He sounded frustrated and I knew the conversation wasn't going to go anywhere. I slunk down in my seat, staring silently out of the window. Jacques liked to tell me I was a champion at sulking, which I adamantly denied, although in my more relaxed moments I could see where he was coming from.

When we had a mini-stand-off like that, he would always come forward first to break the silence and coax me out of my grumpy mood. We both wanted to make up, and we did, but I was aware that we never resolved or even fully discussed how we would bring our two different worlds together.

What mattered, I told myself, was that we both wanted to be together. Everything would follow from that, but it wasn't going to be easy. One of us would need to move countries, leaving family, friends and work behind. It was huge even to contemplate. And Jacques' reluctance to discuss it did worry me at times. Was that because he knew how hard it would be for either – or both – of us? Or simply because he liked to deal with the here and now, while I worried a lot more about the future?

Whatever happened, and wherever we ended up, I knew how lucky I was in Jacques. He had goodness ingrained in him, he was a fantastic companion, and he loved me.

On New Year's Eve Jacques and Dad played with Dad's new wood chipper while I went to ride both the horses. We went out to supper with friends that evening, and then some of my friends came over and we played a card game called Jungle Speed. The idea is that you deal out the cards and then go round the circle one at a time, turning over your top card and placing it on your pile. If yours matches someone else's card, you grab the totem – a small wooden pole about five inches long, which is placed in the middle.

There are very few rules when it comes to grabbing the totem; you can fight, twist and pull to get it away from your opponent and claim the point. It's a bit like an edgy version of Snap, and whenever we played we came away with a few scratches.

Playing with Jacques changed things a bit, though. He was twice as big and twice as strong as anyone else there and more often than not, if he turned over a matching card, his potential opponent would just let him have the totem. So even though he'd never played before, amazingly, he won!

As midnight arrived we sang 'Auld Lang Syne', or hummed it, as most of us didn't know the words. And as the New Year dawned my first thought was, 'This is make or break year for me. Am I really going to make it as a vet? And if I do, what kind of vet work do I want to do, and where?'

I really liked the idea of doing some charity work, so soon after the New Year I contacted a local charity, World in Need, to see if they needed a vet. I knew the director of the charity, and he said they could definitely find a use for

me; I could be really valuable to them in East Africa, helping to teach families to look after goats that had been
donated by Western charities. I loved the idea, and began
to start planning the setting up of a sustainable veterinary
project out there.

For the last few days of Jacques' visit he and I went up
to stay in the house in Welham Green. We wanted to spend
a few days alone together and as all the boys were away, we
had the house to ourselves. We planned to make trips in to
London and cook a few romantic meals, but our vision of a
cosy time together was cut short when we arrived to find
the boiler had broken down. With no heating or hot water
it was bitterly cold, and all we could do was to put on layers
of jumpers (even Jacques felt the cold at this point) and
then snuggle up together.

We had a couple of days out in London and spent our
last day together studying – Jacques worked on his Masters'
dissertation and, with a zoo placement coming up, I did
some frantic mugging up on birds and reptiles.

The time together was precious – we wouldn't be seeing
one another again until after I graduated in July so we were
facing a six-month parting, our longest ever. On our last
night we talked and agreed that, wherever we ended up, it
would be together.

I found it hard every time I had to say goodbye to Jacques,
but this time was awful. I drove him to the airport and we

hugged goodbye, both of us struggling not to cry. Jacques always turned as he headed through security and said, 'You have to go now.' I would turn and walk away, but then I'd turn back and watch him until he disappeared. This time I sobbed, and I was still crying when I got back to my car. The next few months felt very bleak; I was facing several tough months of work and revision, all without him.

I drove down the motorway feeling really dismal, but when I got home there was cheering news. There had been a call to say that Clunky had settled into his foster home and had received medical treatment just in time to save his sight. It was heartening news. Clunky had his happy ending, and I felt sure Jacques and I would, too.

CHAPTER FOURTEEN

Grumpy Lizards and Misty-eyed Gorillas

I had a fair bit of wildlife experience from South Africa, but I wanted to get more exotic animal experience in Britain. I was keen to see what it was like to work with the same animals I'd been around in their natural habitats, and how they had adapted to captivity.

Zoo placements are hard to come by, so I was very excited when I was offered a week's work experience at a local zoo in Kent.

As the zoo was so close to where Ross was studying I went to stay with him for the week. He was in his last year at university and was living in a small house that he shared with a few other students, who never seemed to be there. The house was down a little side road in the middle of a row of terraced houses. It was tall and narrow, with four floors. Ross's bedroom was right next to the communal kitchen, which also doubled as their sitting room and dining room, while the bathroom just off it was the laundry room and shower room. I didn't find this particularly strange as I was used to student houses where limited space meant rooms had to serve several functions. In my second year at university my bedroom was also the sitting room and the kitchen was also the dining room, even though there was barely space for two people in it, let alone a table.

No student house tends to have room for guests, unless they like to kip on the floor, but luckily for me, in Ross's house there was a basement, which they didn't use. I imagined it was going to be cold and damp when he first mentioned it, but actually that's where the heating was, and they had a comfy sofa-bed down there, so I was very happy.

I left early on Monday morning for the zoo. I had no idea how long it would take me to get there, and I didn't feel like panicking while sitting in rush hour traffic, so in the end I was twenty minutes early. I had no idea where to go, but you had to go through the gift shop to get to the park, so I started there. The woman in charge said she'd radio to find out where I should be, and ten minutes later a girl with a blonde bob arrived. She'd clearly run all the way as she was out of breath.

'Jo? I'm Gemma. I'm one of the vets here. And I'm late for the morning rounds. Jump in the jeep with me and let's go. I'll fill you in on the way.'

As we drove, Gemma explained how the days worked at the zoo. The morning round was filled with routine veterinary treatments, such as worming and collecting faecal samples, plus occasional emergencies that had arisen overnight. That usually finished around 10am, when we would go back to the lab. For the next few hours, we would do lab work, which involved a lot of faecal egg counts, and occasionally a post mortem, as it was a requirement for every animal that died at the zoo, even when the cause of death seemed obvious. That would take us to lunch time, when I would be free to walk around the park, or relax for an hour. In the afternoon, we would carry out planned procedures and do afternoon rounds, visiting every department and looking at any animals they were concerned about.

Morning rounds that day began in the reptile house, where there were six small tortoises, a basilisk – a small Central American lizard that has fins on its head and back, and a rhino iguana, which is a huge lizard, about a metre long, with jaws strong enough to break your bones if he decided he didn't like you. Our job was to worm them all with help from the reptile keeper, Dan.

Worming is a routine procedure that has to be done for all animals in captivity, whether they are zoo animals, farm animals, or dogs and cats, because living in a limited space, compared with the wild, means a high concentration of animals, a lot of faeces and, as a result, higher numbers of worms.

I thought we were going to put a stomach tube into the tortoises, as that's generally what's done in small animal practice, but it turned out we were going to inject the wormer into dead baby mice, known as pinkies, which the tortoises would eat. It meant less man-handling, as the zoo's policy was not to handle the animals unless absolutely necessary.

While I understood the principle, and I'm not a squeamish person, the whole pinkie operation was pretty off-putting. But once we'd injected the wormer into the pinkies and dropped them into the cage, those tortoises moved so fast it was extraordinary, gathering around us like a pack of begging dogs.

We also had to worm the rhino iguana. He was called Crunch, and crunch he certainly would do if you got your hands anywhere close to his mouth. Unfortunately there was no equivalent to the pinkies for him – he would need to be handled, and the wormer had to be poured down his throat. This wasn't going to be easy because he was notoriously bad-tempered and didn't like anyone coming into his enclosure. He was fiercely territorial, and I was told to watch from the other side of the wall, as he didn't know me and might get even grumpier if I approached. Given the power of his jaws I was happy to sit this one out. Dan, who was about my age, walked slowly up to Crunch, talking to him softly so that he wouldn't be startled. Crunch's gaze fixed on him as he came closer, and he gave Dan a few head bobs to try to intimidate him. Dan ignored him, moved behind him and with one quick pounce restrained Crunch by gripping behind his head and around his abdomen. Cue Gemma, who had a syringe with a strong metal tube on the end that she had to put down his throat, to squirt in the worming solution. It had to be metal otherwise he would just have bitten through it. As it was, Crunch decided that he wasn't going to play along and clamped his jaws shut. It was a good ten minutes before Gemma could prise them open wide enough to get the metal tube in, while Dan continued to hang on to him from behind, but she managed eventually.

Finally, it was the turn of the basilisk, but he was nowhere in sight. Clearly he had seen what was going on and hidden himself. I was absolutely no help as I didn't even know what a basilisk looked like. I presumed it was a lizard, but I had never seen, or even heard of them before. So I tried to be as helpful as I could, pretending to know what I was looking for, in the hope that if I came across it, it would either be obvious, or it would suddenly move and catch the eye of either Gemma or Dan. They told me, helpfully, that he was bright green, but there was so much green foliage in his enclosure that I had no idea how we would ever spot him. Twenty minutes later we gave up our search and agreed to come back later in the week to try again. Round one to the basilisk.

Although I'd imagined working with tigers and giraffes at the zoo, a lot of my work there was actually with primates. The first of these that I got to know were the colobus monkeys. With their lovely long black and white fur, these monkeys are distinctive. Like all monkeys they live together in groups and are very sociable. A bit too sociable, actually; the monkey population there was growing rapidly, so our job was to put contraceptive implants into some of the younger females. The idea was to cut human contraceptive implants in half and insert them into the primates. This was a fairly new idea and had only recently been tried, but it made sense, as their reproductive hormones work in the same way as humans', and so far it seemed to have been a success.

In humans the implant is slipped underneath the skin on the underside of the arm. In the monkeys we were going to put them in at the backs of their necks, where they were less likely to remove them. To put in the implants we had to anaesthetise the monkeys as there was no way we could handle them, let alone slip in an implant, if they were conscious. Monkeys can bite pretty viciously.

We planned to implant six young females, and by the time we got there the keeper had already separated them from the rest, using a series of doors that led to different sections of the enclosure. The six monkeys were well and truly annoyed that they were now in the small indoor part of their enclosure, with no food, while their friends were still playing outside, and they were kicking up a terrific racket.

The monkey enclosure looked like a giant jungle gym, full of hanging tyres, ropes and branches. The indoor part of the enclosure was specially designed so that people could work with the animals if need be. There was a tunnel from the indoor enclosure through to the vet room where we were, and we were able to isolate each monkey in the tunnel and administer the anaesthetic via a syringe pole through a grating. Once each monkey was asleep, it was carefully lifted from the tunnel onto the table, where the procedure took less than a minute. A small patch of hair behind the neck was clipped, the skin cleaned and the contraceptive implanted through a very small hole made using the tip of a scalpel. The hole would then be closed with sterilised surgical glue and, once we had moved the monkey into the next-door section to recover, the anaesthetic reversal injection would be given. An hour later all the monkeys had been implanted and had woken up. They were all a bit groggy, so they would be kept indoors until they were alert enough to rejoin their friends.

Gemma hoped that it would be at least a year, maybe two, before they had to do the procedure again.

My biggest challenge of the week came when I was asked to do a post-mortem on a dhole that had just died. I'd only just found out that morning what a dhole was (it's a kind of wild dog that looks like a cross between a wolf and a fox), so when Gemma said she was really busy and could I do the post-mortem while she did rounds I was a bit daunted. Would I know one end of a dhole from another?

Gemma laughed and said she was sure I'd be fine. She dropped me off at the shed where the dhole was, with a bag of instruments, and said she'd see me in an hour or two, when she would double-check my findings.

There was nothing for it but to get on with it. A post-mortem is not a question of simply cutting up the dead animal; it's a methodical process, which complements a thorough history from the keeper when a vet is trying to establish the cause of death.

It had been a while since I had been trained to do a post-mortem at college, and my only experience since then had been the post-mortem on the alpaca with Niall. I certainly hadn't come expecting to do one on my own. But I decided to imagine doing a post-mortem on a dog and as I made the first incision it all came flooding back to me.

I quite enjoy post-mortems. I don't mean to sound gruesome, and of course I'm always sad that an animal has died, but I like the idea of solving a mystery. Remember that early passion for forensics? I've always loved piecing clues together.

In the end this post-mortem didn't involve much of a mystery as I came to a conclusion pretty quickly; the dhole had had septicaemia, presumably from a large bite I found on its neck. Dholes are pack animals and the keeper's report made clear that this one had been at the bottom of the pack. It had been picked on by the others, which was terribly sad. There had been a nasty fight about five days earlier, involving this dhole and the pack leader, which this one had clearly lost. The keeper hadn't been aware that he'd been so seriously injured, and I didn't blame him as the hair on dholes is so thick that it completely covered the injury. The previous day this dhole had been much quieter, hiding by himself, and sadly this morning the keeper had found him dead.

This sort of situation creates an ethical dilemma for zoos. In the wild, the animal at the bottom of the pack would have plenty of space to get away from the bullying animals higher up the pecking order, but in the enclosure there isn't enough space to get away. And if the keeper was to remove the bullied dhole, the next in line would take its place at the bottom of the pack.

Removing the pack leader wouldn't help either, as it would dramatically upset the pack dynamics. It's not easy being a keeper and having to make these decisions, and the dhole keeper was taking it hard. He came to join me in the post-mortem shed and he said he'd asked himself whether he could have done any more to prevent this happening. He was deeply upset by the death of one of the animals in his care. Zoo keepers are a dedicated bunch, and they take real pride and pleasure in the well-being of the animals they look after.

The star attractions at this zoo were the gorillas. These extraordinary, gentle and intelligent apes, the largest of all the primates, are also among the most endangered and this zoo was a world leader in their captive management and breeding.

There were three large gorilla enclosures at the zoo, each the size of a square barn several storeys high and measuring at least fifty metres on each side. The gorillas had inside and outside sections of the enclosure, and many levels to live on. There were ramps, ropes and wooden beams as well as plenty of tyres to play with, rope swings to swing on and large hammocks to lie in. The keepers did their absolute best to ensure they had a highly enriched habitat. Their food would be hidden all over the enclosure on all the different levels, so that they had to use their innate skills and look for it.

There were about ten gorillas in each enclosure and each keeper was in charge of just two or three. Gorillas were prized and well looked after here, and it was clear how invested each keeper was in their gorillas. They all had names and individual characters, and just hearing the keepers talk about them made them seem uncannily like humans.

We made lots of visits to the gorilla enclosure, to give the keepers advice on usually very minor ailments. While other departments would ask the vet for advice on obvious problems, the gorilla department called the vet for everything, including minor scratches.

Nothing would go unnoticed, and they received the very best of food and health care. If a particular gorilla seemed a little depressed one day it was an immediate cause for concern. Keeping them well and happy was paramount.

When I was there one of the gorillas had an autoimmune problem with her eyes and she needed drops. The keepers had trained her to tilt her head for the drops when they put a hand diagonally up to the bars. She would tilt her head the way the hand was tilted. As a reward she got her favourite Bombay mix. I was seriously impressed at how clever she was, but I was told it strictly was not a 'trick' and that they only taught things like this when absolutely necessary in order to help the animals.

On my last day we darted a rhino that had some ongoing problems with sores that weren't healing well. The zoo had five black rhinos, which was exciting as I had only ever worked with white rhinos in Africa, although I knew that they were pretty similar. The only difference, according to Jacques, was that the black rhinos were slightly more unpredictable.

Jacques liked to tell a story about when he was working in a game capture team before I met him. They were releasing a black rhino onto a reserve and everything had gone smoothly. The rhino had been moved and woken up and had run off over a hill. Jacques was involved in packing up and was just loading the last bits of equipment onto the back of the bakkie when suddenly one of his colleagues yelled, 'Get in!' Jacques turned around to see the black rhino that had just been released charging back over the hill in their direction. Jacques' colleague had fired up the bakkie and started to pull away as Jacques was sprinting towards it. He dived onto the flatbed at the back and pulled up the tailgate just in time for this rhino to thump hard into where his legs had been dangling just seconds before. It was a story Jacques liked to repeat, to reinforce how dangerous black rhinos can be. Had it been a white rhino, he said, it would have just run off and left them alone, but black rhinos are far more irrational and likely to charge.

The rhino I was dealing with now was in a shed, so was unlikely to charge, although we still had to treat it with great caution and respect. Up close these creatures are awe-inspiring, and I never tired of seeing the size of them or their extraordinary horns.

The sores on this rhino, probably the result of pressure from brushing against the walls of the enclosure or bathing in the concrete-lined wallowing holes, needed to be cleaned and a cream dressing re-applied. The first dart didn't discharge, which was a bit of a blow, as until it discharged, no one apart from the vet in charge could go into the area. The dart contained drugs that were potentially fatal to humans if absorbed into the system, something I knew all too well after my close call with a dart during my work experience in the game reserve in South Africa four months earlier.

The difference in health and safety rules between the two countries was like light and dark.

While the vets in the reserve where I'd worked had been reasonably careful, Thys had loaded the dart with the drugs, without donning safety goggles or gloves, as I stood next to him. I had stepped back and told him that what he was doing was dangerous and he said, with questionable logic, that when he didn't wear safety protection he was more careful.

In England, no one apart from the vets was allowed within ten metres of the drug. As a consequence we had to stand around in the cold while the dart was being loaded and fired, and wait until it had fully discharged.

Finally, after a very chilly half an hour, the dart discharged and another twenty minutes later the rhino became sleepy. Pulling him over was hard. Ropes were put around his legs with about ten of us on each rope, but he was fighting the anaesthetic so we were being dragged rather than making any real headway.

After ten very tiring minutes he finally went over and I was allowed to get up close to him to help with the treatment. He was soon sorted out and back on his feet, but somehow, without having to run through snake- and tick-infested bush surrounded by wild lions and goodness knows what else, it was a different and more mundane experience for me than it had been in South Africa. I had enjoyed my work in the wild so much more. There was more drama, more danger, more adrenaline and excitement – working with the animals in their natural habitat was exhilarating. I realised how incredibly lucky I had been to have had that experience.

Nonetheless, I enjoyed my week with the zoo vets and I would happily have stayed longer. It was nice to stay with Ross, too, and to see a little of his student life. He had a good friend, Becky, and I left my car at her house every day, so on the way home I'd pop in and have a cup of tea with her.

The only downside at Ross's house was the rotten internet connection. So when I got back home on the Friday evening I couldn't wait to talk to Jacques and tell him all about the work I had been doing, especially with the rhino.

Jacques didn't like the idea of animals in captivity, but I take the view that zoos are a vital source of education and conservation. It's undeniable that most people will never see these animals in the wild, or understand how magnificent they are, without zoos.

CHAPTER FIFTEEN

Stella the Heifer

I peered over the pen door and then stepped back rapidly.

Ears back and chin raised, the woolly alpaca on the other side didn't look happy, and I knew what was coming next.

'Lucy, I can't go in there, she's going to spit at me.'

'Don't be daft, she's just a bit worried. Honestly, look how cuddly she is. Just don't look her in the eye, it might alarm her.'

Cautiously, I opened the pen door and stepped inside, while staring pointedly at the wall and not the cross little alpaca inside.

Pffffffpth.

A lump of something green and pungent hit the front of my overalls.

I jumped back out of the pen.

'She spat at me! I knew she was going to. And you said she wouldn't.'

Lucy laughed. 'Well, why do you think I got you to go into the pen first?'

It wasn't the most auspicious introduction to farm medicine week. We were in the Royal Veterinary College's farm department, where they'd just built a hospital ward. Until then the farm department had been forced to share the stables, but now they had their own shiny new ward. Among the first occupants were two alpacas, Coco and Chanel. Coco was a young alpaca, known as a cria, and she had broken her leg. She was a valuable alpaca and her owner didn't want her to be put to sleep, so she had come in to have a metal plate and pins put in. As Coco was so young, and alpacas are herd animals, the farmer who owned her had sent Chanel along to keep her company, and she was the one being decidedly grumpy.

Coco was making a good recovery and in normal circumstances she might already have gone home, but the winter's heavy flooding was still causing mayhem in Kent, so the owner had decided to pay for them to board at the hospital, rather than keep her at home on his waterlogged farm. It wouldn't be good for Coco's leg if she was slipping around in the mud, so she was being treated to a long convalescence.

We had to check on Chanel and Coco every morning, and today it was my turn. Unlike some of the others in my group, especially Lucy and Grace, I hadn't had a lot of experience with alpacas. I had heard that they could be sweet-tempered, easy animals. But Chanel, who was behaving like an over-protective nanny, was beginning to convince me otherwise.

I could see that alpacas behaved a bit like horses, putting their ears forward when they were happy or interested and back when they were upset or annoyed. Chanel was obviously very annoyed, because her ears were almost flat – she was getting ready to spit again.

I backed off until she had calmed down, and Lucy, having laughed at my mishaps with them, offered to teach me how to handle them.

Apparently the proper way to restrain an alpaca is to go up to it and hug its very long neck, which causes it to stand still (probably in the hope that you'll let go), so that a second person can then put a head collar on it, a bit like on a horse. I thought Lucy was having me on when she told me to hug them, but when she finally convinced me she wasn't I followed her instructions, feeling like a complete idiot, and to my amazement it worked perfectly. I can't say that Chanel enjoyed the hug, and to be honest it wasn't my favourite moment either, but she stood stock still as Lucy put her collar on and then led her off. With Chanel out of the way I was able to check on Coco, who seemed like a sweet little thing, a lot more cheerful than her minder.

My encounter with the alpacas was the start of a cheerful and very pleasant week. Having got their own hospital ward, the joke was that the farm department didn't actually have that many cases in to fill it. We expected to have to bridge the gaps with seminars and private study sessions but in fact we were lucky – ours was a relatively busy week with a few interesting cases.

The previous week had also been farm medicine, but for this the five of us in my group were billeted in a large house in Kent. It was a lovely house, but with very little furniture, so we felt we were rattling around in it, living out of suitcases, with nowhere to put anything.

We spent our week out and about on the farms, all of them knee-deep in mud, doing vaccinations and health checks as well as calf-scoring, a system designed by Winconsin University in which you score each calf between 0 and 3 on nasal discharge, eye discharge, faecal consistency, coughing and temperature, to get a total that helps you assess the general health of the calf. We also did a bit of foot-trimming and some James Herriot-style ambulatory calls: seeing individual cows that have specific problems, such as being off their food, or needing a partial foot amputation.

One dark morning Lucy and I got up at an unearthly hour to pregnancy scan twenty cows and synchronise the hormonal cycles of five others so that the farmer would know when to inseminate them. After a very chilly and muddy four hours we spent the rest of the morning sitting in the kitchen trying to warm up over several cups of tea.

That afternoon we went on call-outs with Roger, one of the farm vets from the practice, to farms that wanted us to check over a few cows or needed some advice, but as we drove through one of the very deep 'puddles' in a dip in the road, icy water suddenly gushed out of the glove box onto Lucy's lap. Lucy shrieked, but Roger had to keep going to find a place to get off the road. By the time we stopped Lucy was soaked and freezing cold, and steam was pouring out of the air-conditioning vents. I've never been more grateful for being in the back of a car.

Amazingly the engine was all right and we drove back to the house so that Lucy could change. When we got back to the vet practice, Roger began mopping up the car with towels and having a bit of a panic about how to tell his boss, since the car belonged to the practice. We gave him a hand and after ten minutes spent clearing the worst of it up he decided that the car didn't look too bad, and that he'd keep quiet and hope the whole incident would pass unnoticed. We thought that might be a tiny bit optimistic, given that the front footwell, formerly pale grey, was now a dark sludge colour.

At the end of the week Lucy came home with me and we rode the horses, me on Tammy, who was in a reasonably cooperative mood, and Lucy on Elli, who was good as gold. Lucy loved riding; she'd had lessons as a child and riding for her was always a real treat. Afterwards we went out and looked around the shops before going to a bar for cocktails. I invented an incredible one after sweet-talking the barman into making it for me – orange juice, cranberry juice, pineapple juice and Amaretto. It was delicious. I got him to taste it, and he agreed and even said he might put it on the cocktail list, although he had second thoughts when I insisted he call it 'The Jo'.

Lucy left by train the next morning while I went back to the stables to spend some more time with Tammy and Elli before heading back to Welham Green for farm medicine week. It had been several weeks since I was last there, and I'd missed college and all my friends. As I carried my bag into the house I yelled out to see if any of the boys were home.

James was there, having supper with his girlfriend Hannah, so I joined them for a cup of tea and a chat. I hadn't seen either of them for weeks. They were in the same rotation group and they'd just been on an equine rotation. No sign of Kevin and John, but Andrew appeared later that evening, back from a week working with a small vet practice in his home town.

As the four of us sat and talked it dawned on me that this – my life at college, my student world – would soon be over. Soon I would have to decide where to go and what kind of job I wanted. And I still had no idea – farm, equine, small animal, wildlife? I hoped the coming months would help me to come to a decision. One by one all my friends were making their choices – James sounded pretty certain and Lucy had chosen her next step. She wanted to do farm work and had applied for a farm vet internship. She had a clear vision of what she wanted: a life in the country, work with farm animals and a dog of her own to enjoy the outdoors with her. I wanted that kind of clarity, too, but I wasn't there yet.

That night I lay awake for a couple of hours, thinking about choices and the future. If I graduated as a vet, would I stay in England or go to join Jacques in South Africa? I couldn't imagine being so far from my family, and goodness knows what I would do with the horses, and yet I loved Jacques and I loved the work out in Africa, with animals in the wild, and on the big, dusty farms. Eventually I fell into a restless sleep, still puzzling over where my life would go in the coming months.

The next morning I was bleary-eyed, but a hot shower got me going and I headed off to the farm department to meet the others in my rotation group. I was excited about farm medicine week because I enjoyed farm work and I knew I still had a lot to learn, so I was ready to get stuck in. Although I'd done a lot of farm work with Thys in Africa, that was population health, and what I hadn't done a lot of was clinical one-to-one work with farm animals. One-to-one work is fairly uncommon these days. Most problems are resolved in advance through welfare precautions or are diagnosed at a point where it's not economical to save the animal, but some farm animals do still need clinical treatment – either because their owners don't want to give up on them or because the condition has been caught early enough – and this was our chance to get involved with that side of farm work.

Our first new case was Chicken, a sheep whose full name, for reasons no one could discern, was Chicken Little. Chicken was a chunky older chap belonging to a ruddy-faced farmer who clearly regarded each of his animals as his personal pets. We could only imagine that he'd let a small child do the naming!

'Can you save him?' he asked anxiously, scratching his head. 'I believe we can,' James, the clinician, told him. 'He's got a good chance. It's one of the more common cases we see referred here and we'll do our best for him.'

Chicken had a blocked bladder. Male sheep and goats that are allowed to get fat can easily develop bladder stones that can block the urethra, especially if they have been castrated, because castration removes the hormonal influence that allows the urethra and penis to grow to their full size. The passage that the urethra follows in male sheep and goats isn't just straight from the bladder, around and out through the penis; it goes backwards and forwards in an 'S' shape so the stone can easily get stuck somewhere along the route. When this happens, it blocks the flow of urine and the sheep becomes very ill. It will appear restless, dribble urine, show signs of being in pain and, if the bladder bursts, it will die.

The way to deal with this differs depending on the individual. Sometimes the stone is stuck at the tip of the penis, which can be fixed by cutting off the urethral process at the tip. More commonly, though, we need to take them to surgery to flush out the stone and fit a tube leading out through their abdomen, bypassing the urethra so that the urine drips on the floor through the tube. This process is called a cystostomy, and it allows the inflamed urethra time to heal.

Sometimes the stone has already passed, but the inflammation around where the stone was stuck can cause spasms, which can be treated with medication. This was the case with Chicken. He went in for surgery to have a cystostomy tube fitted and we discovered that the stone had gone but his urethra was very inflamed.

Poor old Chicken was incredibly stoical about the whole thing, but he had clearly been having a pretty miserable time. Over the next few days, as the pain and inflammation cleared, he became much more cheerful, and once his tube had been removed and the opening closed, he was able to go home in the back of his happy owner's truck.

Abigail the Jersey cow had been admitted on the day that Chicken left. She was lovely – a perfect example of a neat brown cow, and with her huge eyes and soft ears she was undoubtedly a glamourpuss in the cow world – but she had a serious stomach problem that is, sadly, all too common among dairy cows.

A cow has four stomachs and the fourth is the abomasum, which, like human stomachs, holds all the stomach acid necessary for breaking down food. The abomasum is small and it normally sits to the right of the rumen, the first and largest of the stomachs, held in place by the rumen's size and weight. If for any reason – illness, a change in diet – the rumen is a bit small, the abomasum, which tends to fill up with gas, can float out like a balloon and get wedged on either the right or left of the abdominal cavity. This is known as a displaced abomasum.

Abigail had an RDA – a right displaced abomasum – and she needed surgery to correct it, otherwise it would kill her. Right displacement is rarer and more of an emergency than left, and most of us in the group had never seen surgery for an RDA, only LDAs, so poor Abigail gave us a valuable opportunity to learn something new.

Diagnosing RDA or LDA is fairly easy. You have to put your stethoscope against the cow's abdominal wall then flick the wall; then, if the gas-filled displaced abomasum is located the other side of the wall, you will hear a pinging sound. We all had the chance to listen to this, and everyone could hear it except me! 'Oh yes, there it is,' nodded Jade, Grace, Katy and Lucy, as each took her turn, but when my turn came I heard nothing.

'Am I being totally useless?' I said as I turned to the others. 'You all heard it right here? Right?'

'Well actually, a little higher up,' Lucy helped. I moved my stethoscope a little higher. 'Yep, there,' she confirmed. Still nothing.

'Seriously, I blame my tools. This stethoscope is useless! Luce, can I borrow yours?'

'Sure thing,' she said as she passed me her bright green stethoscope. I was still annoyed that the purple one I ordered had turned out to be royal blue.

'Nope. Still useless. Urgh, I'm going to be an awful farm vet!' I moaned.

Lucy stepped closer. 'Show me exactly what you're doing.' So I did, and still got nothing. 'You're not flicking hard enough. You literally have to hurt the tip of your finger.'

I tried again. 'Oh my word, I heard it. Lucy, you are a genius, thank you!' I practised a few more times, just to make sure it wasn't a fluke. And no, it wasn't. I had just been too feeble with my flicks.

The surgery, which was done under local anaesthetic with Abigail still standing, involved cutting into her flank so that the vet was able to reach inside and put everything back where it should be. Cows are very resilient and can cope with this, where many other animals wouldn't.

I got the job of giving Abigail the local anaesthetic, a lot of it, injected in an 'L' shape around the incision site to ensure that all the nerves in the incision area were blocked. There's a knack to it that vets have to learn: the needle is inserted, the injection given and then instead of taking the needle fully out, you leave the tip under the skin and draw it along, while injecting more solution, so that you're left with a bubble of anaesthetic under the skin. I hadn't done that before, so I was a little nervous, and very careful, but it worked just fine and Abigail didn't appear to feel a thing.

Lucy and James performed the surgery together. They cut a thirty-centimetre-long incision, got hold of the abomasum, stuck a pump into it and deflated it, before putting it back in place and suturing part of it to the abdominal wall so that it couldn't float again.

Surgery like this is routine, and cows normally make a full recovery, but in the following days Abigail failed to improve as she should have. We were all concerned, and the regular checks on her were increased, but eventually James and her owner took the decision, after more investigations and careful consideration, to put her to sleep.

We all felt so sad as she was such a pretty cow and she should have been fine after the surgery. But clearly there was another underlying health problem which had probably been the cause of the stomach displacement in the first place.

It's always hard for a vet to accept that they can't help an animal and must let it go. You do everything you can to help an animal get well, but sometimes your best efforts just aren't enough, and part of the job is knowing when to stop.

Our next patient was a steer, or at least that's what it said in the name section on the admission forms the owner had filled in. A steer is a castrated bull, so we were a little surprised to find that what we had on our hands was a young heifer. James immediately re-named her Stella – well, it was a bit like steer.

Stella was fifteen months old and she had contracted tendons. One of her hind legs was completely straight and she couldn't walk properly – she walked on the tiptoes of her hind legs and looked rather comical, although the condition was not in the least amusing for the poor cow. It is a congenital condition that a cow is born with and it gradually gets worse, so that by the time they're a year or two old they can barely flex their legs.

Luckily the condition can be corrected with surgery. However, when James sent us into the pen to do what should have been a completely straightforward, standard admittance physical examination, it became very clear that Stella had no intention of cooperating. She ran round and round, with wild eyes and flaring nostrils. Anyone would have thought we were about to lasso her.

Stella had never really been handled before and was clearly very scared. We made a swift exit from the pen and James said he'd do the examination himself. The College, while happy to occasionally make slaves of their students, don't particularly want them getting squashed!

The next day Stella was booked in for her operation and it was all hands on deck. She would need a full anaesthetic, which is quite unusual for farm animals, but she was so wild that there was no other way we could help her; operating on a moving leg certainly wasn't an option. My rotation group was going to do the surgery with James, but the equine surgery rotation group was having a quiet day and was therefore sent over to watch while the anaesthesia rotation group was sent over to do the anaesthetic. So fifteen of us students were in the pen with James, a couple of other clinicians and a rather confused Stella.

Unfortunately she wasn't the only one being temperamental; the anaesthetic machine was playing up, too. After a half-hour delay it was finally fixed, and a sleepy Stella was knocked out with an injection onto a clean straw bed. While operations like Abigail's can be done with the cow still awake and standing, this one definitely couldn't.

Once she was out the anaesthesia team leapt into action and put a tube down her windpipe to give her gas, and we got the go-ahead to operate. I was going to scrub in and help, and I hoped it would involve more than simply holding the instruments.

As James finished cutting the tendon, he turned to me and asked me how I felt about suturing the wound closed. I said brightly that I had every confidence I could do it, so he passed me a needle and the suture material – some strong catgut. The needle, however, was completely blunt and it was the only one we had, so from the outset I struggled to get it through Stella's hide. With so many people looking on it wasn't the time to look feeble, so I clenched my teeth and shoved the needle through, slowly making my way along the fifteen-centimetre incision. I'd closed about half of it when the anaesthetist yelled out that he was turning off the anaesthetic. As James said 'Fine,' I was thinking, 'No, please, I still have loads to do.'

I knew that it meant I had no more than four or five minutes before Stella would be awake, so I tried to speed up. But the needle was becoming increasingly blunt, so the struggle to get it through was tougher each time. As I went in for the last few stitches Stella was beginning to move, so I was now trying to stitch a moving target with a ridiculously blunt needle. With one final push I got the last stitch in just as Stella kicked out and we all leaped out of the pen.

It was such a treat to watch her progress over the next few days. She started to become a little more trusting of people and began to tolerate us going into her pen. But best of all, she was learning to walk properly for the first time in her life. It would take her a few weeks to get the hang of it, but instead of struggling to get around she would now have a happy, comfortable life. Seeing the difference in her left us all feeling that being a vet really was worthwhile.

CHAPTER SIXTEEN

Man's Best Friend

I looked around the crowded waiting room for my next case. To one side I spotted two elderly women deep in conversation, one with a Yorkie at her feet, the other holding the handle of a pink pushchair.

'Mrs Grogan with Rio?' I said.

Both women looked up. Mrs Grogan must have brought her friend along, and a baby as well, by the look of it. I smiled. 'Would you like to come this way?' They both got to their feet and followed me, along with the dog and the pushchair.

In the consulting room I offered them both a seat. 'Now, is this Rio?' I said, looking at the Yorkie.

'Oh no, he's here,' said the woman with the pushchair, unzipping the cover. Two small heads emerged from underneath. 'This is Rio,' she said, lifting one onto the table. He loves football,' she added, by way of explanation. 'And his friend Wayne has come along to keep him company.'

Rio was tiny. He was a miniature Yorkie, rather than a standard one, and on the smaller size of miniatures. He couldn't have weighed more than two kilos. He had hurt his foot when a fireguard fell on it, and the referring vet had bandaged a splint onto his front left leg. On such a tiny dog this unwieldy combination looked almost as big as the rest of him. My heart melted watching him trying to hobble around.

Gently I began to examine Rio, checking all his vital signs, while asking Mrs Grogan exactly what had happened, and when. She was halfway through the story of how Rio had jumped out of his basket by the fire to get his ball and knocked into the fireguard, when the other woman, who until now had sat quietly to one side of the consulting room with her dog, suddenly spoke.

'I'm not sure I should be here,' she said.

'Really?' I looked from one to the other. 'Aren't you together?'

'No,' they both said. 'We just got chatting in the waiting room.'

I blushed bright pink. For ten minutes I'd had someone sitting there who shouldn't have been in the room at all. Why hadn't either of them spoken up sooner?

'Goodness,' I said, hoping I didn't look as embarrassed as I felt. 'Sorry about that. Would you like to go back to the waiting room and I'm sure you'll be seen soon.'

Once she'd gone I turned back to Mrs Grogan, who was stroking Rio and fussing over him.

She finished telling me the story of the accident, with plenty of flourishes and sound effects, and then her lip began to wobble. 'Doctor, will he get better? I can't lose him, I just can't. He and Wayne are all I've got.'

I did my best to reassure her that Rio was in good hands and we would do everything we possibly could for him. Then I left Mrs Grogan with both her dogs while I reported back to Vincent, one of the residents in small animal orthopaedics, where I was halfway through my week's rotation.

Tall, with dark curly hair and the most seductive of French accents, Vincent was one of the RVC's heart-throbs – most of the female students and nurses seemed to have crushes on him. I liked Vincent because he was a really good vet, thorough and very caring. And of course it didn't hurt that I could listen to him talk all day.

He admitted Rio for X-rays so that we could see what had happened and establish if surgery was needed. To do an X-ray we needed to insert an intravenous catheter to administer the anaesthetic drugs through, but this was no easy feat. Even cat-sized ones were pretty big for Rio. I was pleased the film crew weren't around that day, as getting it in was extremely tricky, and I was grateful that I wasn't under the scrutiny of the cameras.

The radiographs weren't good. Rio had clean fractures through all four of his metacarpals (the equivalent of the bones on the back of your hand) on that leg. They were completely displaced and unless we could insert pins he would probably never be able to use the leg again.

Vincent measured the width of his bones on the X-ray on the computer system to work out what size pins would be needed. There was an 'Ah …' and then silence. Rio's bones weren't much wider than 1.5mm, and the medulla, or inner region of the bones, was 0.6mm. As the pins would need to slip into the centre of the bones, that meant we would need 0.6mm pins.

This sent the orthopaedic team into a panic. Did pins so narrow even exist? They would be like the finest sewing needle. Even ultrafine wire is 1mm wide. A hunt began and after a few hours of searching through the large store of sterilised equipment and implants, some minute pins were finally found and Rio was booked in for surgery the next day.

I was due to scrub in for the surgery and I was looking forward to it. At the Queen Mother Hospital there was a surgery preparation routine that everyone followed: check phones and answer messages, go to the toilet, eat a full meal (even if it meant having lunch at 10am), have a glass of water, and let someone know you're going into surgery so that your colleagues (or in my case the rest of the rotation group) don't think you've gone AWOL.

Once you've gone through all of that, it was time to get into your scrubs – an outfit that, while lacking in style, more than made up for it in comfort. The blue scrub top and bottoms felt like pyjamas, and the white clogs were incredibly comfy to wear. An unflattering green hairnet indicated that I was a student (pink for anaesthesia, yellow for visitor, blue for staff), and it was all topped off with a white face mask, which I never liked as it would always slip up my nose into my eyes, leaving a mark over my nose and cheeks that would last for the rest of the day.

Rio's surgery, although technically straightforward, was incredibly complicated and fiddly. As I peered as closely as I could get, Vincent ever so gently pushed each pin down the middle of one half of the bone, and then fed the other half onto it. As the bones were so small, he couldn't use any force at all because they would have simply snapped.

After four tense hours, Rio had four new pins in his broken metacarpals. A post-operation X-ray showed they were well aligned and made him look like a miniature version of *X-Men*'s Wolverine, a thought that made us all laugh. Another huge bandage and a fresh splint were put on his leg, so that even if he wanted to use it, he wouldn't be able to. It was vital that he didn't put the slightest pressure on it over the next few weeks, as the pins were so thin that until the bone around them had fully knitted, they would easily bend.

Rio went home a few days later. Mrs Grogan was over the moon – I don't think I had ever seen someone so happy. She had been convinced he wouldn't be able to have his leg fixed and that he wasn't coming home. She was so weepy, and so grateful, that I just wanted to give her a hug.

I did my best to explain to her the kind of aftercare Rio would need, and when she should bring him back, but she was too busy cooing to him and petting him. So I thought it best to tuck the written instructions into her hand and asked her to read them carefully when she got home. 'Yes, yes, dear,' she said, popping Rio into the pink pushchair, where Wayne was already snuggled.

It was mid-February and I was enjoying orthopaedics. Vets, like doctors, are divided into those that prefer medicine and those that prefer surgery, and for me it was becoming increasingly clear that surgery was more interesting and more satisfying. I really enjoyed being able to fix something then and there, rather than calculating medicines and waiting to see whether they worked.

This was my second week back at the QMH. The previous week I'd been in small animal soft tissue surgery, where we'd been back on those gruelling 6am starts and 6pm finishes, and that's when we weren't on checks, walking all the dogs out to grass and doing meds between 8pm until 10pm. We also had to be on call overnight, and although I was lucky and didn't get called out, I kept waking in a panic, afraid that I'd slept through the phone.

It had been another hectic week, with one case after another coming in for operations, but the case that stood out for me was a super-friendly old chocolate Labrador called Hermes. Named after the Greek God of luck, poor Hermes was anything but lucky – he had visited the QMH thirty-three times in the previous few years with all manner of problems to do with his skin and his gut. His biggest difficulty was that he wasn't holding down food. On his previous visit he'd had a camera inserted into his stomach to investigate and it seemed his exit to the stomach (the pyloric sphincter) was abnormally shaped. So he was back in for a U-Y pyloroplasty, which is essentially a reshaping of the stomach exit in which you make an incision like a U then stitch it back up in the shape of a Y.

Hermes' owners had gone abroad for a couple of years, and one of the staff had offered to foster him. He'd been in so many times that everyone knew him and loved him. And he returned the love; despite all the procedures he'd had, and the fact he was ageing and was a bit arthritic and creaky, he was always so happy to see us. It was nice to have a patient who would wag his tail cheerfully every time you came to visit him.

It was a long and complicated operation in a very hot operating theatre. There were always at least seven of us in there, and the heating was up high, as these animals are unable to regulate body temperature while under anaesthetic, so within minutes we were all sweating. This time we had the senior surgeon, a resident surgeon, a surgical nurse, who gets the instrument from storage if it is not present, the anaesthetist, an anaesthesia student, a student scrubbed in (me) and a student not scrubbed in, taking notes (in this case, Lucy).

I had been given the job of passing the instruments, but soon after the operation started I began to wish I was in Lucy's place, quietly jotting everything down from the safety of the back of the room. Passing the instruments might sound simple, but it turned out to be a sweat-inducing nightmare. Of course, I knew the names of the basic instruments – scissors, scalpel, forceps and so on – but at the QMH there was a bewildering assortment of instruments and they liked to use the proper name of each one. Since most of them had been named after their inventors, it wasn't forceps, it was De Bakeys; it wasn't scissors, it was Mayos, and so on.

Not only that, but I was expected to pass said instrument in the correct way. The surgeon would hold out the palm of their hand, bark out the name of the instrument and I would be expected to slap the handle of the instrument onto the outstretched palm so that they could just close their hand around it.

The surgeon in this operation was one of the more intimidating ones. As he called out the name of the instrument he wanted, I would take a wild guess. Most of the time he'd then snap 'nope' and I'd try again until I got it right. After a couple of rounds like this I was so on edge that I dreaded his next demand. When it came I stared wildly at the tray trying to guess what Adson's was, until Lucy edged into sight and pointed, from behind her notepad, towards a pair of forceps, which I grabbed and handed over, handle first, while signalling 'Thank you' to Lucy with my eyes from behind my mask.

The surgery went smoothly, and once I got past the instrument panic, watching was fascinating, as the surgeon deftly changed the shape of Hermes' stomach exit without adding or removing anything.

By the end of the operation, several hours later, all had gone well and I was so hot I thought I might melt if it went on for a single minute longer. Hermes woke up feeling pretty groggy and I felt so sorry for him. He had been through things like this so many times. But the next morning everything had been forgiven, he was back to his normal waggy self and happy to see everyone. I know if I was taken away from my home and operated on without my consent and without understanding why, I would be terrified and hate the people who had done that to me. It always amazes me how trusting, forgiving and loving dogs can be. I guess that's why I'm a dog person at heart.

Over the next few days Hermes made good progress. He was a valiant old dog, and despite his age he was full of life. By the end of the week he went home, with plenty of pain medication and on a very delicate diet, but with the potential for a few good years ahead of him. Before he left he did the rounds of the staff, giving each of us a final lick and a wag goodbye.

At the end of each day Lucy and I did the evening checks together. The students often worked in pairs, as it made everything a bit easier and a bit more fun. The checks would take at least an hour, usually longer. Every dog had to be taken out into the sludgy patch, medicines had to be administered, and vital signs – temperature, heart-rate, gums, breathing – had to be checked. You can tell a great deal from a dog's gums – you can pick up signs of anaemia, jaundice, dehydration and lowered blood pressure. You press the gum with your finger and a healthy gum will go from white to pink within a second or so after release. And finally, when we had done all the checks we had to fill in the kennel sheets for each dog, detailing everything that had been done.

I was just coming to one of the last dogs, one that both Lucy and I had been avoiding. I sighed. 'Luce, can you come and help me with Bruno?'

'Urgh, fine. I thought I had got away with avoiding him!'

Bruno was a very large, young, bouncy German Shepherd. Every time his kennel door was opened he would barge out, sending everyone flying. To top it off, if you did manage to lasso him with your slip lead as he came shooting out, it wouldn't stop him. He was so strong that he would just drag you wherever he wanted to go. Taking him out was becoming a two-person job.

Lucy blocked the kennel door as I squeezed in and got a lead on him. Then she put her lead around his neck, and we walked him outside together, just about managing to keep hold of him between the two of us. He'd come in as an emergency a few nights earlier, and he'd needed surgery after swallowing a Batman toy, but he was clearly not feeling unwell anymore and we were hoping he was going to be discharged any day.

In the end Bruno went home on our last day in small animal soft tissue, and after the long hours and endless checks on multiple animals I was glad to be moving on. In orthopaedics we wouldn't have to do the same checks, and that alone made the following week look extremely attractive. In fact, I was home by six most evenings, which was an unheard-of treat, and gave me time to talk to Jacques, whom I was missing like crazy, and to put my CV together and start sending it out to recruitment agencies. Like all the other student vets I was keenly aware that once we graduated we would need to find jobs. I still didn't know what I wanted to do long-term, but as I was planning to spend some time working for World in Need in Africa I decided the best thing would be to start by looking for locum work.

In locum work I would hire myself out, on a short-term basis, to vet practices that were short of staff or needed to cover holidays. It meant I would have plenty of flexibility, which was just what I needed, although I was feeling quite daunted by the idea of having to hit the ground running.

By this time most of my housemates had a pretty good idea of what they wanted to do.

Kevin had gone off the idea of being a vet, but still wanted to work in the veterinary industry. He was missing the sun of South Carolina and would be going back to the USA after graduation, so he was veering towards finding a job as a veterinary pathologist, which would essentially be doing post-mortems all day long and taking samples to look at under the microscope to determine causes of death. It wouldn't be everyone's cup of tea, but Kevin had a very forensic mind and it would suit him. As for John, he always knew he wanted to work with small animals in general practice and his heart now belonged to Britain, so he was in the process of sorting out his visa so that he would be able to stay. James also was pretty sure that small animal practice was the direction he was heading, but as for location, that was going to be largely influenced by his girlfriend, Hannah. He kept telling her 'anywhere but Wales', but she was ignoring that and had been investigating small animal and mixed practices in several locations, including Wales. Andrew, though, was hugely undecided about where he wanted to be and what he wanted to do long term. But, like me, he hoped that as we progressed towards the end of our university days things would become clearer.

In my last couple of days on orthopaedics I was assigned one of my saddest cases. When I went to collect the file containing Shadow's history I could see that the dog had been slightly lame in her left front leg for the last six months, and there had been a mysterious swelling appearing and disappearing around her elbow. So far the diagnosis was unclear, so Shadow had been referred to us for tests.

I went to collect Shadow and her owner, Mr Jeffreys, from the waiting room to take a more thorough history. Shadow was an unusual-looking dog: almost orange in colour with the body and face of a Staffordshire bull terrier, but with slightly shorter legs and pointy ears.

While Shadow wasn't the most glamorous of dogs, it was impossible not to warm to her because she was so nervous that her entire body was shaking from head to toe. She clearly didn't like coming to the vet one bit, and she needed a lot of reassurance and gentle handling.

Her owner, a man who gave the impression that on any other day he might have been quite tough, held her in his arms, giving her cuddles and comfort. He wasn't able to add a great deal of new information to what we already knew, so I went to talk to Vincent, the clinician in charge of the case. After coming to look at Shadow, Vincent decided that she should be admitted for a CT scan so that we could have a clear look at what was going on in her elbow.

Mr Jeffreys, who clearly adored his dog, was upset at having to leave her with us. There were tears in his eyes as he hugged her goodbye. I knew that without him Shadow was likely to be even more nervous, and as I led her down the corridor to the surgery ward she shook more than ever, and kept straining to turn and follow her owner. I hoped that, given a little time, she would feel calmer and would be able to trust us, but it was going to be an uphill task.

I found her a large kennel and went to get her several pillows and teddy bears to keep her comfortable until her CT scan later that afternoon. Whenever I had a spare moment during the day I went and sat with her and comforted her as I could see she was still terrified.

Finally, towards the end of the day, she went for her scan. She was put under anaesthetic for it so at least she had a break from her fear for an hour.

I was never good at reading CT scans, which are in 3D rather than the usual 2D X-ray pictures, but even I could see that there was a soft mass behind her elbow. A needle was inserted into it to take some cells for the lab to analyse, but as it was the end of the day it would mean an overnight wait for the results.

The next morning we looked at the cell analysis; Shadow had a mast cell tumour and, due to its position on her elbow, it was inoperable. I had seen a diagnosis like this before and I knew it had been a possibility in her case, but I felt so distressed when I saw it that I became tearful. Shadow was such a lovely little dog, and with her nerves, all I wanted was to try to make everything better for her. It was heartbreaking to discover that she had cancer.

Vincent let Mr Jeffreys know over the telephone, and understandably he was very upset, but he was able to offer him some hope. Although the tumour couldn't be removed, Shadow would be transferred to the RVC's oncology unit immediately to start chemotherapy to shrink it, and if she responded well she might go into remission for weeks or even months.

As I cuddled her goodbye I promised myself that I would check back to see what happened to her. We were changing locations and medical rotations every week or two, and that made it very hard to follow the longer-term cases we handled. All too often I would work intensively with an animal and then have to leave, not knowing the final outcome of the story. I wasn't due back at the QMH until my neurology placement, six weeks later, but in Shadow's case I did manage to pop in before that to find out how she had done. I was delighted to hear that she had responded well to chemotherapy and the tumour had shrunk. She was back home with Mr Jeffreys, to enjoy some precious time together.

CHAPTER SEVENTEEN

Horse Sense

By mid-February, a year into rotations, I was finally beginning to feel like a proper vet. I didn't have to ask how to do things any more, my confidence was growing day by day and I was itching for more responsibility. And during my two weeks' work experience at a big equine veterinary practice and hospital, I got it. The cases came thick and fast, and I was given the chance to get really involved in the treatment and surgery.

First up was a cute little cob foal called Murphy. Only six months old, he had a gentle nature and was more hair than pony, his glorious thick mane flowing down his neck and over his eyes. He'd been put in the isolation block over concerns he might have strangles, a horribly infectious respiratory condition. He was really struggling to breathe well and he had an awful cough.

The mystery was solved when we discovered ugly white ascarid worms in his faeces. Ascarids are a species of roundworm picked up by horses when they are grazing. They're huge – we picked out worms the size of a ballpoint pen – and they can migrate from the intestines to the lungs and cause serious damage and respiratory problems. The horse coughs up the worms, which causes scar tissue in the lungs and permanent irritation. Most owners de-worm young horses and ponies to protect them, but Murphy had been abandoned and taken in by the rescue charity that sent him to us, so he hadn't had all the usual precautions.

The problem was easily sorted with treatment to kill the worms, and Murphy, who had been a bit glum when he came in, soon began to cheer up as his lungs healed and he felt more comfortable. Sam and Amy were with me filming on this placement, and when they found out about the worms they insisted we do a very staged bit of filming where we placed a worm on top of a pile of droppings, and I had to act surprised and say, 'Oh my word, look at that worm,' then pick it up and show it to the camera.

I made a face at Sam. 'Really? You think it will look convincing?'

'It'll be great, really funny,' he insisted. 'Just look as surprised as you can.'

We placed the worm on the droppings, I stepped forward to pick it up and Sam zoomed in with the camera. I was about to go into my routine when the two stable girls decided it would be hilarious to attack me with it. They grabbed the worm and came after me with it and, to Sam and Amy's delight, I shrieked long and loud.

'Lovely, that's even better,' Sam said, grinning. 'But it's in your hair now, Jo, in case you hadn't noticed.'

There are some truly disgusting moments in a vet's life, and this was one of them. With what I felt was impressive control, especially in view of the laughter all around me, I got the worm out of my hair, dropped it on the ground and headed for the loo to wash my hands and redo my hair.

When I got back Sam had composed himself. 'Shall we try that again, Jo? Perhaps you can pick it up with gloves this time. And we'll keep those two,' he indicated the still-giggling stable girls, 'out of the way.'

Also in the isolation block that first week were an emaciated mare and her foal. They had been sent to us by a rescue centre, whose staff had collected the pair from a field where they were found alone and abandoned and in a very poor condition after being reported by a member of the public. The mare had profuse watery diarrhoea, which could have been caused by a number of things, but they were in the isolation block because of the risk that it could be salmonella. We were more concerned over cyathostomins, though, as it was the time of year when they tend to appear. Cyathostomins are parasites of the gut that stop food from being absorbed and consequently cause horses to starve to death – which would explain their thin condition. We had to worm both mare and foal and give them biosponge, an anti-diarrhoea treatment, by mouth several times a day. However, the mare really knew how to kick. Before we could grab her headcollar, she would swing her rear end around and double barrel with both back legs. Her foal was learning pretty quickly, too, so trying to treat either of them was a perilous business.

We felt very sorry for them both; they'd probably been mistreated and had no trust in humans. But we had to find a way to treat them, so, with some of the stable girls, I developed a strategy; we went in with a wheelbarrow as a shield so that when the mare kicked she would strike the wheelbarrow. Once we'd calmed her and got hold of her headcollar we could approach the foal. We kept the head-collar on her all the time as otherwise we knew we would never get hold of her again without it.

There was a security camera in the corner of the stables, and whenever it came to treatment time everyone in the office would place bets on how long it would take us to get hold of the two of them: two minutes, five minutes, ten minutes? Most of the time even twenty minutes was opti-mistic and, as we skirted round the extremely nimble mare, cowering behind our wheelbarrow like a couple of Michelin men in our full isolation kit of overalls, gloves and foot-cov-ers, the staff in the office sat around the camera enjoying the entertainment.

It was worth all the effort, though; mother and foal grew healthier, they put on weight and they did begin to calm down, just a fraction. By the time I finished my two weeks they were due to go back to the rescue centre, from which they would hopefully find kinder owners.

The staff at the hospital included Paul, the head clinician, who threw me in at the deep end. He encouraged me to scrub in, and even to do some surgery, give anaesthetics and take a consult or two. One of these was a pedal osteitis case (infection of the bone in the hoof), and Paul quizzed me in front of the owners about what I wanted to do about it. When he agreed with everything I said, I was on fire!

Another vet I worked closely with was a resident called Evan. We'd met before, when he came to do a rotation at the RVC in pathology as part of his residency. This happened to be at the time I was doing my pathology rotation, so I had spent a week getting to know him over some post-mortems. I liked Evan. Tall and blond, he was young and energetic, and he always had a big smile on his face.

About halfway through my placement I was sent to shadow Evan for the day. Sam and Amy had tagged along, too, with the cameras. I'd forgiven Sam for the worms incident and I was glad to have them along. They'd seen so much by this time that Amy was starting to joke that she could be a vet student, and every now and then there would be an outburst along the lines of 'Yes! I actually understand what that is!' or 'Do you mean he has tachycardia? Yes, that's right, I used a vet word!'

Evan said he had an event horse coming in. It was performing poorly, slowing down and generally seeming out of sorts, and the owners wanted to know why.

When he arrived I was in awe. Rocky was magnificent; a huge, proud horse with a glossy, dark brown coat and black mane and tail. His head was the size of my upper torso and he strode in so powerfully that you could hear him coming from the other side of the hospital. Evan had suspicions that he might have gastric ulcers, which are common in high-performance horses and horses that are quite highly strung. The plan was to put an endoscope down into his stomach to have a look, and Evan was going to let me do this. I was a little worried as I had only passed a scope down a horse's throat once before, and I had never steered one once it was inside, but I was keen to have a go.

Before we could sedate Rocky for the procedure, Evan listened to his heart – standard practice to ensure that it's safe to administer sedation. This normally takes a few seconds, but Evan continued listening far longer than that, and as he listened his ever-present smile faded. I'd never seen him look that worried before.

Eventually he looked up and spoke to Rocky's rider. 'I'm not too happy about the rhythm of his heart. Let's trot him up to see if it changes.' The rider, a tall man in his thirties, who was clearly very fond of Rocky, led him into a trot outside.

Sometimes horses' hearts sound abnormal at rest, but arrhythmias can go away with exercise, particularly in large, fit horses with slow heart rates. That was what Evan was hoping would happen. But after trotting up and down for a few minutes, Rocky's heart rhythm hadn't changed.

Evan decided to wire Rocky up for an electrocardiograph (better known as an ECG) to check exactly what was going on with his heart. The ECG would record the patterns of his heartbeat on a graph. While everything was being set up I listened to Rocky's heart. It sounded like wobbly jelly – all the beats were completely out of sync. I tried to explain this in front of the camera, but in the end the easiest thing was to sound it out: 'boom, boom,' long pause, 'boom boom boom,' short pause, 'boom.' Amy, chuckling away, tried to hide behind Sam so as to not distract me while I was going through my routine.

The ECG gave us the answer. Rocky had atrial fibrillation, a condition common in humans as well as in horses, which causes irregular and often very rapid heartbeat. Normally the heart contracts and relaxes to a regular beat, but when there is AF the upper chambers of the heart quiver instead of beating effectively to move blood into the lower chambers. AF doesn't affect the horse much when it is at rest, but it affects it enormously during exercise. If the heart isn't pumping properly the horse can't function well and will become tired. There is also a small risk that it can progress to a more seriously irregular rhythm, which could dangerously affect the health of the horse and, in rare cases, cause death.

Luckily for Rocky, there was a cure. But it was not without risks, the cure being a drug that would poison him. It was called quinidine (not to be confused with quinine, in tonic water) and it had to be administered by stomach tube every couple of hours for up to seven doses. More than seven doses was deemed too dangerous, because at that point the drug could potentially kill him. It was a case of weighing up which was the lesser evil: the risk of death due to the heart problem or the risk of death due to the drug to treat it. The third option, unthinkable for a horse as magnificent as Rocky, was that he would be put down as he was no longer fit for his purpose.

Rocky's rider and owners needed to think about which course of action to take, given the risks involved, so he was taken home.

A few days later, having decided to opt for treatment, they brought him back in. Evan handed over to me for the first step, which was to place a catheter into the jugular vein in Rocky's neck, which I managed incident-free and which felt like an achievement since it was in front of the cameras.

Meanwhile, Evan passed in a stomach tube and taped it to Rocky's head collar. It looked a bit like a snorkel.

The first dose of quinidine was given via the tube, and nothing happened. No side effects and no change in the continuous ECG we had running. If the quinidine worked, at some point Rocky's heart would quite suddenly convert to a normal rhythm and begin to function normally. We waited two hours before giving him another dose. Still nothing. This went on all day until it came to 6pm and time for me to go home. By then Rocky was on his fifth dose, and still nothing had happened, although he was looking more and more miserable.

I didn't blame him. He was in an unfamiliar place, and he was being starved and poisoned. He must have felt very sick. We kept things light-hearted, guessing what time his heart would convert to a normal rhythm overnight, but as we all dispersed it was clear that everyone was worried.

I spent a restless night and I went in early the next morning, to be met by Evan's tired face and most cheerful smile. That meant Rocky had made it; his heart had converted and he hadn't died from the medication. Evan explained to me it was only after his seventh dose that he had finally converted, at around midnight. Thank goodness! Unfortunately he had developed a rather distressing side effect. Rocky had started having muscle fasciculations – violent twitches – over his right foreleg and neck. His muscles had been jumping around for so long that he was really hot to touch, and he must have been in a lot of pain due to the lactic acid build-up that this kind of twitching provokes.

We spent the day dosing him up with as much pain relief as possible, as well as calcium and other minerals to help his muscles calm down. It took a while, but three days later Rocky got the all-clear to go home. His rider came to pick him up and was over the moon. Although he was employed to ride Rocky and didn't own him, it was clear how much affection he had for the horse.

A few months later the TV crew went to film Rocky being exercised at his yard. It was lovely to see him, and I couldn't believe what an amazing recovery he'd made. He had come back from near death to become a superstar athlete again.

Meanwhile, I got my chance to have a go at some surgery. Paul told me I could castrate a stallion. I had performed castrations before on other animals (remember the boars in South Africa?) as well as on some young colts, but this was a proper surgical procedure on an adult horse, under full anaesthetic, on the operating table.

Stallions are usually castrated at eight or nine months old, when it's easier to operate on them, and the procedure is often carried out in their own stables under heavy sedation. This one was older, however, and he had very well-developed testicles and needed to be knocked out. It was a far more sophisticated surgery than the boars, though. Instead of using emasculators, everything that was going to be left in was tied off with sutures, before the testicle was cut off using a scalpel. The reason why this isn't done when operating in the stables with younger horses is that it increases the risk of infection, since the procedure isn't being done in a sterile environment. But as this procedure took place in an ultra-clean and sterile surgical theatre, the risk of infection was much lower than the risk of bleeding and sutures could be put in.

Next on my list was a hernia case. A hernia is a defect in the abdomen wall, which allows the abdominal contents to fall through the muscles of the abdomen. The last thing you want is for the intestines to fall through because then they can become strangulated. But in this case the horse was young, about a year old, and he had a small hernia, so only some of the fat around his belly had fallen through. It needed closing, though, before it got any worse, and Paul was happy for me to go ahead and open the skin over the hernia, then push everything back through it and close it up under his supervision. Job done!

At the end of every day at the hospital I went home feeling great. I loved horses, loved surgery and enjoyed working with Paul and Evan and the rest of the team. Evan, in particular, taught me a lot. Some clinicians consider students to be a nuisance and some love to teach. He was one of those that loved to teach, so it was a real pleasure to shadow him. He would get me fully involved, explaining and describing what was going on at every stage.

One afternoon he asked me if I had passed a stomach tube before. I had seen several vets do it in the past and had held the swinging heads of unhappy horses that didn't like what was being done, but I had never actually passed one myself. So Evan invited me to do one on a young horse called Ace that had come in the previous night with impaction colic.

I leaped at the chance. The difficulty in passing a stomach tube up a horse's nose and down into the stomach is that you need the horse to keep its head still. It's a procedure usually done without sedation, and some horses, unused to the hospital and the people and procedures, get frustrated and keep shaking their heads. Ace was one of those.

As the tube passes along the inside of the nose, even if the horse keeps its head still, it is very, very easy to hit the small bones in the nose that are covered with blood vessels, and if you accidently hit them you can cause massive nosebleeds.

That's what happened when I passed the tube up Ace's nasal passage. The blood vessels opened and blood streamed out of his nose. And as it did he shook his head and snorted, so that within minutes the whole stable looked as though there had been a massacre.

I was mortified, but Evan was kind, reassuring me that it happens regularly to even the most experienced clinicians. 'Have another go soon,' he said. 'Let's do a swap. After all I'm much better at doing the procedure than holding a horse while it's done so I probably haven't helped.' He passed the tube and double-checked that there wasn't any build-up of ingesta or fluid in the stomach, before pouring fluids down the tube to try to soften and budge the impaction. He needed a repeat of the fluids a few hours later, and this time Ace was significantly better behaved. Evan allowed me to pass the tube and, to my relief, this time it went fine.

To be fair, Ace really was a grumpy horse. During the next couple of days he started defecating again, a sign that the impaction had moved and broken down, and I was allowed to walk him out to graze. Each time I went to put him back in the stable he planted his feet outside the door and refused to budge. It took four or five people, pushing and yelling, to get him back into his stable and, in the end, most of the time a stable hand had to push his behind with a broom to get him back in. If there was no help around, however, I could just about manage to get him in on my own by reversing him into the stable and pushing his chest, so that before he knew it he was in his stable.

At the start of my two weeks Paul had asked me if I wanted to be called out if there was an overnight emergency surgery. I was based at home, only half an hour away, so I had said yes please.

One evening the phone went at around 10.30pm. There was a horse with colic and it was in a lot of distress, Paul said. If it ended up having to go to surgery, did I want to come? I said absolutely. The next call was at midnight, the surgery was going ahead, would I like to help?

I leaped into my car and shot back to the hospital. By the time I arrived at 12.45am the horse was just being prepared for surgery.

It was a young pony called Sunny, just eighteen months old and dun – a black mane and tail and a sandy body. He was in a great deal of pain as his intestine had become displaced and had flopped around into the wrong part of the abdomen. When a horse has displaced intestines, the whole digestive process slows down, so it's very common for them to have an impaction at the same time, and poor old Sunny did.

I scrubbed in and Paul started operating at about 1.15am. I was able to help with the anaesthetic and watch as Paul cut a hole in a healthy part of intestine, got a hosepipe and flooded it with water, then took the hosepipe out and milked out the half-digested matter from the intestines through the hole. The intestine dangled outside the body and a lot of sloppy stuff went into a big bucket. Once it was all out, Paul put everything back in place and sewed it all up. It was impressive, and it was all over in an hour and a half.

I got home at three, slept for four hours and was back at work by eight the same morning. We had to put a stomach tube into Sunny a couple of times a day after that, because his intestines had become very inflamed and were not really moving properly, and as horses can't vomit there was a risk of a build-up of fluid in his stomach if we didn't remove it. It was no fun for him each time, but he put up with our administrations with resignation and within a few days his insides were working efficiently again and we were able to start taking him out to graze on the end of a rope, several times a day.

I was sorely tempted by an invitation to apply for an internship at the equine hospital for after I graduated, but while I would have really enjoyed working alongside brilliant vets like Evan and Paul, and working with horses, in the end I decided against it. I knew I wasn't ready to settle into a permanent job yet. I wanted to travel, and to try working in different practices for a while. I was accepted, subject to graduating, by a locum agency, which meant I could work for a few months after graduation and save some money. I wanted to go to Africa with World in Need; I loved the idea of teaching people in remote villages how to look after their goats. I smiled, remembering Doris the goat, propped on cushions in the back of the SUV. Whatever lay ahead for me, it wasn't going to be tending to goats like that.

I had the idea of taking goat 'goody bags' out with me, and putting the basic care kit for goats in them – a hoof trimmer, a rubber teat to bottle feed, some plastic gloves and a basic healthcare guide. Whenever I had a minute I contacted charities, asking whether they would donate towards the cost of the goody bags, and I struck gold with the British Goat Society, which offered a generous donation, and the World Veterinary Services, which offered to sponsor some of the drugs I might need.

Gradually a clearer picture was beginning to emerge. And as my equine placement ended, so did three months of monsoon-like rain, and the sun came out. At last.

CHAPTER EIGHTEEN

Luca the Great Dane

He was huge. Absolutely enormous. In fact, closer to the size of a pony than a dog. Luca the Great Dane was the largest dog I'd ever seen. He was also one of the softest; a sweet-natured, soppy giant.

Luca arrived at the QMH during the first week of neurology, my final rotation. Neurology is an area of veterinary medicine that can be heartbreaking because many of the animals that arrive in the department are in a bad way. Quite a few of them have spinal problems and need to be carried, which isn't normally too difficult; they're either carried in someone's arms or put on a trolley. But three-year-old Luca, who arrived as an overnight emergency, posed a challenge. His back legs had collapsed and he couldn't walk, but at eighty kilos, or twelve and a half stone, he was far too large for any of our trolleys and too heavy to lift onto one even if he had fitted.

The problem with Luca's spine might have been a slipped disc, a spine deformation, or even a tumour compressing on his spine. An MRI scan was needed for a proper diagnosis. But to get Luca to the induction room for his general anaesthetic required seven people: two to run ahead and open the double doors, four to help Luca along, holding his back end up in a harness, and one to follow behind with a mop, clearing Luca's pee and poo as we went. Whatever was affecting his legs had also left him incontinent, which meant he left an unsightly trail everywhere. And being so big, he produced waterfalls of the stuff. But, to be honest, by this stage of my training I had been covered in a variety of noxious bodily fluids so many times that I barely noticed it any more.

Once Luca was under, we had another problem. He was too big to fit through the tunnel of the MRI scanner. It had been designed for humans, although most dogs fitted into it comfortably. Not Luca. It took a great deal of repositioning, holding bits of him down with Velcro straps and bending his legs, to get him through. But it was worth the effort because the scan gave us the answer to his problem; one of Luca's vertebra had tunnelled into another, causing a compression of his spinal cord. It's a condition called lumbosacral stenosis, or LSS, and it's a problem that happens fairly often with large dogs, giving them considerable pain.

The only way to relieve Luca's discomfort and to allow him to get his movement back was for us to perform a dorsal laminectomy, in which the top of the vertebra, where the compression is, would be removed. So Luca was gently woken and manoeuvred back into his kennel, given plenty of painkillers and left to rest overnight. The following day we took him into surgery.

I had been warned that it would be a long operation, so I prepared by eating a vast breakfast, shovelling down extra toast as I flew around the house getting my things together, and then I drove to the hospital. I was still munching when I arrived.

Getting Luca onto the operating table was the next challenge. He just about fitted, once six of us had lifted him on, but there was great concern that he could easily slip off, so we kept the level low and tied him securely on with straps.

The incision into his spine, made by resident vet Gareth, my supervising clinician for the case, was extraordinarily deep. It honestly looked as though we were cutting him in half. But once we reached his spine it was a really absorbing and fascinating operation. I knew that, unless I chose to be a specialist in this field, I would probably only rarely see an animal's spine exposed, so it was an opportunity to learn. Gareth's skill in cutting off the bone that was compressing Luca's spinal cord was impressive. He had to be so precise;

any major damage to the spinal cord could mean Luca might never walk again.

In the end the operation lasted five and a half hours. By the time we finished the seven of us in the room were hot, exhausted and very, very hungry. But it had gone well – now it was just a question of careful nursing and crossing fingers, toes and paws that Luca would make a full recovery.

The day after the surgery, however, Luca appeared depressed. He was whining pathetically and looking at everyone who passed him with his huge, droopy, sad eyes, so I decided to go and sit with him in his kennel. It was actually much comfier than sitting in the tea room as he had nice squashy pillows and blankets, so I decided that I would tackle two birds with one stone; get some revision done and keep Luca company whenever I had a bit of free time. I think he appreciated it; he kept flopping his head with his drooly jowls onto my lap.

Exams were looming frighteningly close, and nerves were well and truly setting in. It was already almost April and the first one, the practical exam, was scheduled for the week after I finished neurology, so I was revising in every spare minute I had. The practical exam was a horrendous obstacle race of at least thirty timed challenges, with five minutes for each, all different, all involving solving a problem or identifying something. Just thinking about it made my stomach flip.

Luca was one of those rare cases that got under my skin. His big, solemn eyes, floppy jaws and lumbering body made me smile, and his gentle nature touched me. We spent a lot of time together on the floor of his kennel; me propped on the pillows, Luca propped on me, my revision papers propped on his head, as bit by bit he grew stronger.

We managed to get him back onto his feet, lifted by a hoist in a special harness, the day after his operation. I had to scour the hospital for a harness big enough, before eventually finding one in some far-flung cupboard. It was vital that he started to use his back legs as soon as possible, and although he couldn't yet hold his full weight on them, he did well and the movement he managed was promising.

Over the next week we continued with his rehab, and as he started to get better he discovered that even though he couldn't get up himself, he could crawl pretty effectively across the ground. After that, every time I opened his kennel door I had to be careful, because a 175-pound beast would hurl himself through it. Several times he managed to barge his way out and combat-crawl halfway along the ward, where he would stop and try to get everyone's attention. It was extremely funny to watch.

After ten days he was finally able to get up by himself and walk almost unaided, although he was still a little wobbly. Everyone was delighted with him; the operation had been a complete success, and his balance and mobility would improve with time. He was ready to go home.

Luca's owners, a lovely family, were extremely happy to see him. They made a big fuss of him, thanked us profusely and promised to spoil him. After the discharging consultation I walked out with them to their car. It was a black London cab, which Luca stepped into as if he were a fare. He plonked his rear end on the seat while keeping his front feet on the floor. It was hilarious. Luca had been an amazing character and one of my favourite cases. He had a huge personality and he kept everyone amused. He was also a real trouper; he went through a very tough time very bravely. I was glad he had such a loving home, but I was sorry to see him go. I was going to miss my revision buddy.

I'd picked neurology as one of my elective subjects because it was an area I felt I didn't know enough about. Before I started I was nervous and spent a lot of time in the weeks running up to the rotation reading over all my neurology notes. But I needn't have been so worried, as it turned out that the neurology team were really welcoming. They didn't expect us students to know much when we first started, which took a weight off my shoulders as most other rotations expected a lot from students. In neurology they were more focused on teaching a subject that they were really excited about, and trying to inspire us to take a career path in neurology. I was pretty sure I wouldn't be going down that route – disorders of the nervous system were not what set me on fire – but I was glad of the opportunity to learn more about it and work with a nice bunch of people.

To my surprise, neurology was hugely busy. In most other departments we had looked after around four animals a day, but here I had up to seven at a time. Right from day one I was piled high with cases.

My first was Sergeant, a springer spaniel whose owner, a rather timid man, said Sergeant had collapsed. On careful questioning it seemed that Sergeant collapsed like this about once a year. I reported back to Gareth. 'What kind of condition can cause a dog to do that?' I puzzled.

'Laziness,' Gareth laughed, after he'd thoroughly examined Sergeant. 'There's nothing wrong with him. He just can't be bothered.'

Sergeant's owner accepted this, probably because it came from a specialist. Plenty of animals came to the QMH with conditions their first-opinion vets had already diagnosed, but which the owners wouldn't accept until a specialist confirmed it.

Gareth, who had a place on the QMH unofficial list of hottest clinicians alongside Vincent and a select few others, was a dedicated vet who treated animals with great skill and care. Like so many others at the hospital he put in ridiculously long hours, just to make sure that his patients got the best possible treatment.

The day before I arrived he had operated on Fifi, a very sweet black miniature poodle. She'd had a few disc prolapses and was recovering from surgery when she was put under my care, and I had been told she would need lots of special attention and post-surgery rehabilitation. Fifi's was a dramatic case as she had come in after losing all function in her back legs. Tests confirmed that she could barely feel them; when her toes were pressed she didn't respond at all. This loss of deep pain perception meant the prognosis wasn't very good. When I was shown her pre-surgery MRI scan I was shocked. The spinal cord usually looks like a light greyish line running through the vertebrae, but in Fifi's case the line showing the spinal cord was compressed by three separate prolapsed discs and it looked as though it had almost been cut into sections. Her owners were told that even after surgery, which would be costly, she might never regain her ability to walk, but they loved her and wanted to give her the best possible chance, so with their blessing Gareth went ahead and operated.

Now we were at the tense post-op stage, waiting to see how far Fifi would recover. The physiotherapist was spending a lot of time with her, and since I was checking on her every couple of hours I got the opportunity to learn a bit about dog physiotherapy, which was both useful and fun.

As the days passed Fifi surprised the whole department. Not only was she starting to regain her deep pain sensation, she was also trying hard to move her back legs. Every few hours either the nurses or I would take her for a walk in what were known as her 'silver pants' – a support that wrapped around her back legs and had two long handles so that we could hold them up while she walked with her front legs. We gave her lots of praise and encouragement, and it took me back to the start of rotations when I was in the dermatology room wondering who on earth those crazy people were outside the window making all that noise with a dog. Now, I knew it was the neurology department helping a patient to walk again. And it was working. Fifi, responding to our every encouragement, wanted to play and she was already starting to move her legs rather than dragging them.

Tilly, another of my cases, was a fluffball of a dog, a little white Pomeranian with a tiny, foxy face and beady eyes, who was undergoing chemotherapy for an inflammatory central nervous system disease. Her spinal cord and brain had become inflamed but we had no idea why. The condition is known as MUO, meningioencephalitis of unknown origin. When this happens chemotherapy drugs seem to help. Poor Tilly was in the midst of her treatment, so she was feeling pretty rough and looking like a cuddly toy, flopped in her small kennel, so I kept a very close eye on her.

My fourth patient that first day was Billy, a gorgeous whippet who had a haemorrhage into the spinal cord from a car accident and who was recovering with rest and anti-inflammatories. But the case that touched my heart most was Herbie, a Lhasa apso, an unusual, long-haired Tibetan breed. His hair trailed along the floor behind him. Herbie was blind and although they didn't look at all alike, he reminded me of Tosca, who was also coping stoically with her blindness, and who had been such a stalwart and loyal companion throughout this tough year of rotations. Every time I went home Tosca was waiting for me. When I sat reading or revising she sat with me, and instead of disturbing me with her usual demands for attention she'd simply put her head on my lap, or sit on my feet, giving me quiet, comforting support.

The film crew loved her, and we had a lot of laughs over the fact that one of the newer members of the crew was also called Tosca, particularly when we were talking about something silly Tosca the dog had done and someone only caught half the conversation.

In Herbie's case a scan revealed that he also had an inflammation of the central nervous system, which in his case had caused his optic nerves to swell. I was glad of the opportunity to see for myself, as eye diagnoses were one of my weaker points. In this case the problem was obvious and I could see that Herbie's optic nerves were swollen.

They usually look like a cream circle at the back of the eye when you look through an opthalmoscope, but Herbie's were massive and bulging inwards. He was put on the same treatment as Tilly for MUO, a type of chemotherapy that decreased the inflammation in the nervous system.

Herbie started to make a good recovery, and like most of my other patients went home before the end of my two weeks there. But like all chemotherapy patients he would be back many times over the next few months for repeat treatments.

All my patients behaved with remarkable fortitude and restraint, until I met Kevin the cat. Kevin had come in with facial twitching and odd behaviour, and he took an instant dislike to me. Every time I went near him he tried to bite me, which didn't make doing his regular checks any easier. It turned out that his worst problem was his heart, so before he could inflict any more puncture wounds on my hands and arms he was transferred to the cardio ward where I could only hope that whoever looked after him would have better luck.

A few days into my first week Gareth asked me if I could give him a hand with an emergency case, a crossbreed called Casey who had a slipped disc and was now dragging his back legs. He was a tough little dog; he looked a bit like a beagle, with floppy ears and a habit of tilting his head to one side as if he were thinking.

He was in a lot of pain, so we operated that afternoon. Once again it was a long, hot four hours in the operating room, but by the end Casey's disc was removed and there was every likelihood that he would make a full recovery.

My final case was Bertie, a Staffie who had collapsed. If I'm honest, with the exception of Clunky, who stole my heart, Staffies weren't my favourite dogs. With their square frame, barrel chests and squashed faces, they aren't exactly cuddly. But I know that, like most dogs, they can be loving, sweet-natured and loyal, and I decided I should get to know them better, not least because Jacques often said he'd like us to get one in the future.

Bertie was a brave little ambassador for his breed. Like all the dogs who found that they suddenly couldn't walk, he must have been very frightened and confused. But he was patient while we sedated and scanned him, and thankfully we found that his was a treatable condition. Bertie had a fibrocartilagenous embolism (FCE), otherwise known as a spinal stroke, where an embolism had blocked the blood supply to a small part of the spinal cord, meaning the cells in that area could not survive. As a result Bertie's left back leg had become paralysed. He was lucky, though, as it could have happened higher up in his spinal cord, which would have meant that all four of his legs would have been paralysed. With rest, gentle stimulation, anti-inflammatories and physiotherapy he had a good prognosis, and the clinicians hoped he would make a full recovery in four to six weeks, most of which he could spend at home, with regular visits back to the hospital for hydrotherapy and physiotherapy sessions.

By the time I came to the end of my fortnight Fifi was ready to be discharged, to continue her rehabilitation at home. She was able to stand without the support of the silver pants, and although she wasn't yet walking without aid, she could lift up each back leg and confidently place them back on the floor without stumbling. Her owners were delighted. They knew she might be a little wobbly for the rest of her life, but after the initial bleak prognosis she had done so well. I had grown close to Fifi and when I went to see her off I found myself feeling a little choked up. I was so proud of her for pulling through.

On my last day at the unit I brought in cakes for everyone. This had become a ritual for many of us on rotations, to say goodbye each time we moved on. However tough the rotation had been it marked the ending in a nice way. And when it came to leaving neurology, I was genuinely sad.

It was good to go home for the weekend, to catch up with my family and do a bit of frantic revision for the practical exam, which was now days away. Dad was a real help with that. He'd patiently helped me revise all through my A levels and the vet exams at the end of each year, putting up with my mini-tantrums and last-minute panics, and reassuring me that I'd be fine. We had a system; I would explain something to him, and if he understood it then I trusted that I knew it. He sometimes joked that he would probably be able to work as a vet, too, by the time I graduated.

The practical exams were known as the oskeys to us. This was our version of OSCEs, although what the letters stood for I never knew. In fact, the exam had just had its name changed to OSPVEs, but everyone ignored that.

Many of the five-minute tests were pretty simple – washing my hands, taking an X-ray, doing a consultation with an actor who played the part of a pet owner. Others were much harder and I messed up a few. The dermatology microscopy station was hard. I had to identify two slides. On one of them I found demodex parasites, tiny mites that live on the hair of dogs but don't generally do any harm. Phew. But the other was hard to identify. I needed a much higher magnification of the microscope, but the high-power lens wasn't working well and I couldn't see a thing. In the end I made a random guess and went for cocci bacteria. It could have been anything, though.

Then there was the horse leg bandage. I can bandage a leg just fine, but because I had to do it quickly I kept dropping the bandage, and it sprang back and smacked the model horse on the other leg with a thud. But worst of all was the sheep tip. For this one I was sent into a stable with eight sheep in it and told to catch a specific one, tip it over and examine its udder. I spent four of my five minutes running around after a sheep that was clearly annoyed at being tipped multiple times through the day and was not playing any more. I actually pulled a muscle in my arm when tackling it, but I had to ignore the sudden surge of pain that shot up my arm and push on, and in the last minute I managed to get the sheep over and do a quick examination.

By the end I felt wrung out. And this was just the start – there were five more exams to go, each one as terrifying as this first. It was hard to imagine coming out the other side without my brain being fried and my nerves shredded.

CHAPTER NINETEEN

The End in Sight

By Easter, which fell in early April that year, we were all revising for finals. Two months to go and suddenly I felt as though I knew nothing. I couldn't remember one end of an animal from the other. I felt as though I had somehow been getting away with it all this time, but I was about to be found out. How had I ever thought I could really be a vet?

It wasn't just the non-stop revision that was worrying me. I'd always thrown myself into everything, but now I was beginning to regret getting involved in so much. Why had I taken on planning the graduation ball? And offered to be in the Final Year Revue, appearing in the sketches as well as being in the band? And agreed to be in the TV series? Hadn't I realised that all these things would be coming to a head at exactly the same time that my future career was hanging in the balance? Clearly not, but it was too late now. I didn't have a spare moment, from waking to crawling back into bed again. It was turning into a mad, mad month, and May was looking even worse.

This wasn't the right moment for ITN to start insisting on last-minute filming sessions, and they were very apologetic that it was coming at a bad time, but they were still missing a lot of footage so we were summoned to film the opening sequence, some studio shots and more linking scene shots. We also had to have press photographs taken and film more of what they called the master interviews – one-to-one interviews with each of us that they slotted into the films.

For the opening sequence ITN had hired a vast studio and brought in lots of animals. Since I was one of the few horsey people I had been given the horse to hold. His name was Barron, known as Baz, and I felt really star-struck. He was famous, having appeared in *Downton Abbey* and *Pirates of the Caribbean*. But despite his sparkling credentials he wasn't an easy partner to deal with. The crew had decided to put out bales of hay in the studio for us to sit down on or stand behind. Baz and I were supposed to walk in and take our place to one side, behind the bales, but every time we appeared he would drag me to the hay and shove his head down for a munch. We must have done close to twenty takes before the producer was happy.

The studio shots were also in a hired studio, but this time they were filming each of us individually, with animals.

For this one I got an obese ginger cat that was moulting, and I kept sneezing and needing tissues. Despite this, Isobel, the producer, kept insisting on retaking shots of me putting my nose on the cat's nose then bringing my head up to look at the camera. By the end I looked like an allergic mess, face red and eyes streaming.

The linking shots were less fun. I had to walk in and out of the QMH so many times I lost count. The reception staff kept laughing every time I came in through the doors and stood and waited for them to close so that I could go back out again. Putting my bag in a locker was another sequence that took many takes, as they filmed this remarkably unexciting event from every angle. It didn't help that the first time we did it I walked in and tried to open my locker, but found that it was stuck. I was trying for ages, and finally I gave up and asked Sam to come and help prise open the locker. Rob was standing behind Sam in hysterics, almost crying at how incompetent I looked, and insisted that was a blooper shot. I wasn't impressed. And finally, the master interviews, which were always filmed late in the day in the clinical skills centre after everyone went home. This meant filming took up a whole evening, but the bonus was that we got free pizza.

While it wasn't easy fitting all this in, and some of it was pretty tedious, for the most part I enjoyed it because I had become good friends with the film crew. In fact, I was dreading the end of filming because I'd grown to enjoy their company; we'd shared a lot of laughter together over the many mishaps of the past year, and I was beginning to think that I might actually feel quite bereft without their constant presence.

It wasn't time for goodbye, though, as we'd be seeing them for results day in July and then once again for our graduation. I didn't dare think about that, however, as it all seemed a lifetime away.

Graduation would be a couple of weeks after results day, and two days after that we were holding a graduation ball – our final event of the year. When we set up a graduation ball committee we decided that whoever found a venue would head the organising committee. I decided to check out Hatfield House. I went for a tour, took lots of pictures and put it to the committee. They loved it, so suddenly I found myself chief planner for a party for 300 people with a budget of £25,000.

Slightly horrified that I'd put myself in this situation, I had hastily delegated jobs to everyone, hoping they'd sort out all the details, like flowers and tickets and photographers and entertainment. But despite my best efforts to get all the others to do the hard work, I was forced to roll up my sleeves and do some of it myself. It was extraordinary just how much was involved – we'd had numerous meetings and looked at endless menus, samples and pictures, and we still had all kinds of last-minute decisions to make, from the pre-dinner drinks to the food to the flowers.

Most important of all, I needed to find a dress to wear. Jacques had promised to come over for my graduation and to come to the ball with me, so in between revising the anatomy of pigs and potential causes of fits in dogs I scoured the internet for a gown that would magically convey the grace, style and poise I felt the occasion merited.

The ball would be held in July, as our final event, but the Final Year Revue – a stage production with a mixture of singing, stage acts and pre-filmed videos, was to be performed over two nights in early May. A college tradition, the Revue was a chance to let our hair down, take the mickey out of ourselves and party before the final push towards the exams.

I'd put myself forward for a *Game of Thrones*-style Veterinary Oath skit, a 'What does Mark Fox say?' dance, (a play on the 'What does the Fox Say?' YouTube hit, in our case involving an elderly parasitologist called Mark Fox), a choir, the band and a 'derm-emergency' video, the point of which was that there was never an emergency on dermatology.

The *Game of Thrones* act was the veterinary oath we would all have to take once we had qualified, spoken while wearing surgical kit, in a parody of the show's famous oath, addressed to a tree with our vice-principal's face on it. Both that and the 'What does the Fox Say?' skit went down a storm, as did the shot challenge – a film of several students downing a shot for every letter you have after your name as a fully qualified vet: BVETMED MRCVS. So twelve shots. And astonishingly, most people afterwards were still standing! I thought it really reflected the many years of the attitude of 'work hard, play hard' that my peers had adopted throughout their degree. Clearly their stomachs had learnt to take it. I gave it a miss, though.

The Revue was a fantastic success and sold out on both nights. For the second night we had hired a DJ for a big party at which we enjoyed all the spirits left over from the shot challenge.

At the party I was thrilled to catch up with Kate, one of the friends I had lost touch with over rotations because of our wildly different schedules. She lived nearby and in the early hours we headed back to her place. My housemates had all dispersed to other people's houses for the night and the trains had stopped running, so I was grateful for her offer of a bed.

We got in, sleepy-eyed, but decided to stay up for some toast and a cup of tea and a chat. It had been such a good night, but I suddenly realised that, apart from the graduation ball, this had been our last party as a year group. I felt a moment of real sadness – I had loved being a student and in five years together we had all become very close. Now it was almost time to go our separate ways.

With the Revue behind us it was time to put all thoughts of partying aside. Throughout May I was attending lectures from nine to five each day, and revising or filming each evening. And although I'd started my revision in good time I still felt completely overwhelmed by how much I had to get through. I had eight full, large A4 folders, four textbooks and a research project with associated published papers to read through. There were moments when it was difficult not to panic.

The first of my exams, a couple of weeks before the others, was an oral exam on my research project. I was very proud that I'd pulled off the project after the initial doubts of two of my clinicians, and I felt it had been really worthwhile. I found that shoes do change the shape of horses' hooves, generally for the worse, although there are pros and cons with both, and my conclusion was that horses are better off without shoes. This was a controversial conclusion that some in the equine community wouldn't like. But it was also a real contribution to the ongoing debate. My supervisor had been delighted and had suggested I submit my paper for publication in a scientific journal.

I knew that because it was controversial the examiners would give me a complete grilling on every aspect of my research, and because of this I had prepared thoroughly. I had gone through my research with a fine toothcomb to find any tiny flaw and to prepare a response to it. Going into the exam I felt very nervous, but I came back with a decent response to every one of their many questions. I had a tactic to not let them push me to be biased, because I knew that if I showed bias they would rip into that. So whenever I had an opportunity I made sure I discussed the pros and cons of both shoes and barefoot management. I didn't feel I'd been caught out, although they'd certainly tried.

Two weeks later it was time for the written exams. We had four: an extended matching questions (EMQ) exam, a long answer exam, an elective exam and a SPOT test, which is like a timed multiple-choice exam.

In extended matching questions you have five clinical scenarios and ten answers, and you have to match the scenario with the correct answer. The questions were along the lines of, what is the diagnosis? What diagnostic technique would you use? What would the treatment be? You could use each answer more than once, so there was no chance of narrowing the choice of possible answers.

The long answer exam was essentially a problem-solving paper. We were given lots of clinical scenarios, and we had to say what we thought about each of them and the process you would go through to diagnose and treat the problem.

The third paper was split into two parts. The first was a published scientific article that we had to critically analyse and say whether we could trust the results. The article we had was a badly written one on the effects of passive smoking in dogs. I thought it was quite interesting, but I knew there were massive flaws in the experiment that was being written about, so I had lots to say. The second part was based on one of our electives and we had a choice of questions. I chose an equine soft tissue question: a colt has come in to be castrated – talk through how you would go about this and include any complications that might arise from it.

The final exam was called the SPOT test and it was a multiple-choice exam held in the lecture theatre. We had to watch a PowerPoint presentation that kept on moving from question to question every minute. You had to write your answers, and there was no going back and no changing them, so the pressure was full-on. You either knew the answer straight off, or you didn't.

All of the exams were tough. I was counting on lots of horse-related questions but, apart from my elective question, many seemed to be about small animals – really hard ones requiring information we would never use in first-opinion practice. I was also counting on getting an ethics-based question in the long answer paper, as I could waffle on about things that were common sense, but no, they were all clinical.

By the end we were all tired and very uncertain about how we'd done. Lucy was taking the healthy attitude that what was done was done, and nothing more could be done about it. Charlie was back to his normal bouncy self, hugging everyone that seemed to be fretting about their results. Katy was feeling pretty happy with her answers. She had always been a genius, though. And Grace and Jade? Well, they were pretty focused on finding a glass of wine – pronto.

But there was at least a welcome distraction. In return for our participation in the series, ITN had hired an enormous bouncy castle and brought in caterers to cook everyone paella for lunch. It was the perfect antidote to the tension and stress of a week of exams.

And finally, it really was all over. I could hardly take it in. After all the frenzied activity of the past few months, there was nothing to do but wait for a hellish two weeks until results day. I felt lost! I went back home for one of those weeks, spent time every day with Elli and Tammy, packed away my books and files and mooched around, biting my nails and trying to distract myself. Abi came riding with me a few times, filling me in on her new boyfriend, an old friend of hers from Exeter University who had recently moved to the area. I was so happy for her.

In the second week I went back to college to finalise some things for the graduation ball and to spend a few relaxed evenings with Lucy, cooking and watching *Star Wars*. I had never watched the original movies, and she insisted we had to do it right now while we had a bit of time.

The day before results day I made a deal with Dad. ITN wanted to film me getting my results, which meant waiting to go and find them on the board at the RVC, rather than looking them up earlier online. Dad agreed to look them up online and text me if I had failed, so that I would at least know in advance.

That evening, back in the house, James, John, Kevin and Andrew were all waiting just as anxiously as I was. It was strange to be in the house together. The five of us had rarely coincided over the past year, but that evening we had dinner and sat around chatting and laughing about the good times we'd spent together and how all five of us were so different, yet perfect as housemates. We would all be moving off in entirely different directions soon. It was almost the end of an era.

The next morning I woke ridiculously early, tried to get to sleep again, gave up, had a shower, got dressed, paced around, tried to eat breakfast, felt sick, and finally headed to college.

I knew the online results would be posted at ten that morning, and of course most people would look their results up in private before facing anyone else. But for those of us in the series there was no such luxury. But as ten came and went there was no text from Dad. That had to mean I had passed, but I needed to see it for myself. What if Dad's phone had failed? What if he'd tried to text me and it hadn't got through?

The film crew couldn't meet me until midday. They needed to film all ten of us and I had to wait my turn, but it was beginning to feel like an exercise in extreme cruelty. And when they did finally pitch up they suggested we go outside to do an interview first. What? I was desperate by then, but they insisted. I had absolutely no idea what I was saying in the interview.

Finally we were done and they followed me over to the board with the results pinned up on it. But my mind had gone blank. What on earth was my candidate number? It took me a minute to remember, and once I did it was another very tense minute as I searched for it amongst 250 others. When I found it and read across the page I did a double take. 'Rotations = Merit, Research = Merit, Exams = Merit, Overall = Honours'. I stared at the page. It said Honours. I had achieved Honours, the equivalent of a First Class degree. It hit me with a tidal wave of emotion, and I broke down and sobbed. Kate arrived at that moment and I was grateful for a hug. I had planned to stay cool, especially with the cameras there, but after the hardest, most stressful five years of my life I was done. I was a vet. And I would never have to take another exam again.

* * *

Jacques had arrived a couple of days before my graduation ceremony, and after a six-month break it was wonderful to see him. Our relationship had survived the parting and now he was here for me, for the most important day of my life.

He sat with my parents and Ross in the Central Hall, Westminster. It was scorching and like the other graduates I wore a heavy black gown – I don't think I've ever been so hot. The staff were handing us glasses of water and watching anxiously to make sure that no one fainted.

It was a long wait in the wings for my turn. I was number 100 out of 250 and I could only feel for the person who was up last. As my name was called, Joanna Nevison Hardy, I crossed the stage, applause ringing in my ears, beaming with pride. I handed my hood to the president of the RVC who, in keeping with tradition, placed it over my head and onto my shoulders, gave me a wink and said, 'Enjoy your moment,' before the vice-president handed me my certificate and they both shook my hand.

When it was all over, and family photos had been taken, ITN did a final shot of the ten of us jumping in the air. And naturally they made us do it thirty times. After which, they gave us each a huge frame with two pictures inside: a black and white shot of me from my studio photo shoot and a colour picture of the ten of us from the filming of the opening sequence. I was sad to see them go, and I would truly miss them. We hugged them goodbye, not wanting to let go, before heading off for champagne and celebrations.

My family had a lot to celebrate, because both Mum and Ross had passed their finals, too. Mum had got a degree in Humanities with Creative Writing from the Open University, and Ross had graduated from Canterbury Christ Church University with a degree in Music. Dad was beaming with pride while joking that the only degree he held was from the School of Hard Knocks.

Two days later we had our graduation ball in Hatfield House. It all came off to perfection: gorgeous gowns, Pimm's on the lawn to the sound of strings, delicious food, flowers and music. I wore a dusty pink chiffon floor-length dress by Lipsy. I felt so elegant. And Jacques was with me. It was the first time a lot of my friends had met him and it felt really special having him there.

The next morning I packed up all my things and moved out of the house in Welham Green and back home. I hugged all the boys – I would seriously miss them. They had all passed their exams, and now James and Hannah, along with Buddy, were heading to Wales where, despite James's lack of enthusiasm, Hannah had landed a job. Kevin was moving back to the USA, where he had got the job he wanted as a veterinary pathologist in Georgia. John, determined to stay in the UK, had got a job lined up in a mixed first-opinion practice in Scotland. Andrew was still undecided, so he planned to take the summer off before looking for a job. Lucy had passed, too, and she had a highly sought-after farm vet internship in West Sussex that would lead to a job. She was only going to be forty-five minutes from my home, and we promised we would keep in touch and see each other as regularly as possible. In the two weeks between exams and graduation she had bought a gorgeous black cocker spaniel puppy that she called Renly, after the character in her favourite *Game of Thrones*, and I was looking forward to lots of puppy cuddles each time we met up.

Charlie, Grace, Jade and Katy all passed, and they were all still looking for jobs that were either small-animal based, or in mixed practices with minimal equine work. They were all quite happy to take their time and enjoy a few weeks of well-earned holiday before starting work.

As for me, after a couple of weeks' holiday, I had some locum work lined up so that I could save some money before heading out to Africa for a few months, first to work with an animal charity near Jacques in the local South African townships, and then in Uganda as a farm vet with World in Need.

After the packing up, the goodbyes, the tears and a hot fifteen minutes trying to find a way to stuff everything into my car, it was time to go.

I was a fully fledged vet and a whole new life was just beginning.

Acknowledgements

I would like to thank all my friends, family and colleagues who supported and encouraged the creative process of this book in some way or other. In particular, I would like to thank David Church, Vice Principal of the Royal Veterinary College, for being so enthusiastic about the story and giving it his blessing on behalf of the RVC. I would also like to thank Lucy Jerram for being a great friend by my side throughout the whole 'Rotations', both in the good times and the bad, and for being happy for me to share her story in this book. Further, I want to thank ITN Productions for casting me in *Young Vets*, for believing in me to do them proud on national television and for providing me with the opportunity to open doors I never thought I would open. I would also like to thank my wonderful editor, Caro Handley, for being someone I feel I can talk to about anything, for clicking with me from day one and essentially holding my hand into the literary world, which was so unfamiliar to me. Finally, I would like to give my biggest thank you to my parents, Giles and Clare, and my better half, Jacques, for supporting me through the most challenging five years of my life when I was trying to obtain a world-class veterinary-medicine degree from the best vet school in Europe, for picking me up when I wanted to quit and for celebrating with me in my successes. I couldn't have done it without you.